# the myth

# of aid

the hidden agenda
of the development reports

# the myth
# of aid

the hidden agenda
of the development reports

Denis Goulet
Michael Hudson

**Prepared by the Center for the Study of
Development and Social Change**

An IDOC Book
IDOC NORTH AMERICA
432 Park Avenue South, New York 10016

Co-Published By
ORBIS BOOKS, Maryknoll, N. Y. 10545

Library of Congress Catalogue Card Number 77-146247

## TABLE OF CONTENTS

## illiteracy in america

America is profoundly illiterate, and the time is long past when we can shrug off the prophets who are telling us so. One of those prophets, Daniel Berrigan, recently a fugitive *for* justice, diagnosed our national condition in these terms:

> America, that America which presumes to speak for you and me in the world at large, and for God as well, and for the human community of this point of history–that America is literally illiterate with regard to the meaning and value of life. Fully four-fifths of our 200 million fellow citizens–beginning with the men who wield the most power over us, and continuing through the universities, the legal institutions and even the churches–are simply illiterate. With respect to the available text of our world we are roughly in a state equivalent to that of the Northeast Brazilian *campesinos* in respect to theirs. [1]

It is only out of a profound illiteracy that we can spend five hundred million dollars in Laos in a war that is not only undeclared but secret and call the government agency which does so our Department of "Defense." This expenditure constitutes almost five times the total annual income of Laotians, whose per capita income averages a pitiful ninety dollars per year. Beyond the deaths and maiming, nearly one-third of that country's notably gentle people are compelled to seek survival by becoming refugees.

Last July, Ambassador B. McMurtire Godley was prompted to voice his regret to the Senate Foreign Relations Committee when this situation was discussed in closed session. Yet, since we had to think of our boys in South Vietnam, he added, it was "better" that Laotian families should take the "punishment" instead of American soldiers. The use of "better" and "punishment" in this context betrays a failure to connect words with reality which is not only illiterate but inhuman.

The same inhuman illiteracy is operative in the "concern and goodwill" perpetrated by the United States on the nations of the Third World in the form of "development aid." By now the second development decade has commenced, and it threatens to be a second decade of underdevelopment. In spite of the noble sentiments, the rhetoric is unreal. The Third World will continue to be controlled by those who are said to be developed, and human degradation will increase–unless radical changes take place in the perspectives and values of the developed.

Again it is the question of word and meaning. The United States is "developed": one nation, comprising six percent of mankind's total population, continues to devour over fifty percent of the world's resources. It rejects basic change internally or externally while gorging itself mindlessly. Repression at home and abroad inevitably spreads to nightmarish proportions, as men become increasingly aware of the structures of violence that treat them as expendable objects. This is "development."

If life is to become more humanized for all mankind, affluent and poor alike, it is urgent that prestigious "development" blueprints formulated by spokesmen for the powerful be subjected to an immediate process of de-mystification. Their crippling assumptions must be exposed. Documents such as the Pearson and Peterson Reports examine problems of underdevelopment as if there were no causal connection between the predicament of the deprived nations and the "development" of the dominant nations. The authors of these reports do not question the worldwide market and military system which is essentially a system of control over the dominated nations. They propose either changes that are relatively trivial and do not threaten the governing system, or else more basic ones without any serious mechanisms for their implementation. In either case, the order and stability which is based on present power relationships remains the acknowledged major deity.

Such documents are evil in their nature and antihuman in their effect. They contribute to the contemporary Western obsession with death at the precise historical moment when life-loving creativity is desperately required. But this is not to suggest that their authors are generally less than intelligent men of good will. It is again a question of a peculiar kind of illiteracy. Products of the system they defend, they diagnose and prescribe from within, lacking a sense of the broader realities of history. By accepting a commodity view of man, within the parameters of Pax Americana, they render their best contributions to the world's sense of direction sterile, counter-productive, and finally deceptive. By failing to make justice the basic guideline they deprive the word *development* of all moral significance.

If there is to be a possibility of choosing a human path so that *all* men may become active subjects of their own history, it must begin at the level of a new analysis. Fortunately, a small number of thinkers in the dominant societies are now beginning to speak a language which is more and more similar to the language of Third World thinkers and formulating a sharp new conceptual framework. In the dominant societies some of these thinkers, especially the blacks and the chicanos, have found themselves to be in very much the same situation as the people of the Third World. Together they are learning much about alternative development possibilities in such diverse countries as Cuba, Tanzania, Yugoslavia, and the Peoples' Republic of China. Instead of merely sharing an apocalyptic vision, these men increasingly present a more comprehensive and realistic explanation of the present world situation and propose concrete ways in which the tragedy can be transformed.

Fundamentally they identify two contradictory languages about underdevelopment. The first view postulates that while some nations are unfortunately "backward" they can evolve in the direction of the "developed" nations, if they adopt acceptable behavior and "modern" goals. They too can "develop" if their efforts are supplemented by some generous aid and transfers of technology along with more favorable modifications in the ongoing international system. This conceptual system is embraced by the dominant nations and international bureaucracies in general, and by the Pearson and Peterson Reports in particular. It follows the classic liberal tradition. It is non-threatening and presents no serious problems of guilt or historical responsibility.

The *second view* rejects this language as historically unreal. Underdevelopment is not rooted in providence, inferior personality traits, or traditional values. Rather it exists because the Third World has been the object of systematic subjugating action by the dominant nations. Following centuries of colonialism and neo-colonialism, a worldwide system has been "aided," "technologized" and "mutual-securitied" into place.[2] The privileged classes of the Third World have had their capacity to control and exploit buttressed so that the powerless serve the powerful while subsisting at their pleasure.

However, for a host of reasons, the repressed consciousness of the Third World has at last begun to emerge with a mounting insistence on throwing off the status of dependency and subservience. Having been "discovered" and then manipulated, the Third World is now discovering for itself that the history it has learned was written in the language of its oppressors. And so there is a mounting drive in the Third World to reject the language of "development" invented by the "developed" and spoken by its own privileged classes to stave off the day of reckoning. Insurgent voices throughout Africa, Asia and Latin America, like blacks and others in America, vehemently speak words like *liberation* and

9

*justice,* rather than *aid.* The concern of those who speak this new language is to *be* more rather than to *have* more.

The Center for the Study of Development and Social Change, through its members, conducts independent study on the issues of underdevelopment. The Center sees itself as a "liberated zone" where critical men of all "worlds" can reflect together, denouncing in order to announce. Its goal is to contribute to the contemporary struggle which aims at enabling all men to become more. Hence it is with great pleasure that the Center has accepted an invitation from the editors at IDOC, who share similar ideals, to provide current studies for this particular book. Both IDOC and the Center see the present moment as one when men everywhere must join efforts to move our lives in new, more human, directions. As a prerequisite, all men must be challenged and encouraged to develop a critical capacity for reflection.

Appropriately, the authors of the two studies comprising this book know the meaning of praxis–the unity of action and reflection. Both are among the new voices which America desperately needs to hear.

Denis Goulet is the only American presently specializing in the Ethics of Development. He has worked closely with Louis Lebret, founder of IRFED *(Institut de Recherche et de Formation en vue du Developpement)* in Paris. In addition to laboring as a factory hand in France and Spain, Goulet has lived with Bedouin tribes in the Sahara and primitive Indian populations in the Amazon. He has also served on development planning teams in Lebanon and Brazil. After obtaining his doctorate in political science at the University of Sao Paulo in 1963, he has taught at several universities, Indiana, Saskatchewan, California. He is one of the founders of the Center for the Study of Development and Social Change. He has written widely in several languages. His first book in English, *The Cruel Choice: A Normative Theory of Development,* will soon be published by Atheneum.

Michael Hudson is an assistant professor of economics at the New School for Social Research in New York City. He received his doctorate from New York Universtiy while working as a balance-of-payments analyst for the Chase Manhattan Bank. He is a protege of Terence McCarthy. Among his publications is *A Financial Payments-Flow Analysis of U.S. International Transcations: 1960-1968* (New York University, G.B.A., Institute of Finance: *The Bulletin* Nos. 61-63, March 1970). His contribution to this present volume will appear as a chapter in his book on *The*

*Economic Consequences of American Empire* to be published by Holt, Rinehart and Winston in autumn 1971.

In the present work, Goulet and Hudson, from the vantage points of their respective disciplines and life experiences, attempt to lay bare the implications of the reports prepared by the Pearson, Peterson and other commissions in recent months. The veritable flood of such reports indicates, perhaps, a troubled conscience among the powerful. In any event, the emerging consciousness of the Third World cannot be trifled with, though for a time at least autonomy can be denied by brute force. Therefore, just men need to perceive reality and opportunity clearly at a moment in history when man must become more important than "security," stability or profits.

We believe that the analyses and recommendations of our two associates contribute toward genuine action on behalf of man. So-called traditional moral authorities in this country have evidenced little capacity for effective leadership. It seems fruitless to remind them of the ancient directive of a man (named Paul) that "justice and holiness are born of truth." They have, for the most part, internalized a view of the world which at the deepest levels does not differ from that of contributors to "View # 1 Reports."

It would seem then that our hope can only rest in the people. Only if they become sufficiently convinced can we move beyond the stage described by Daniel Berrigan:

> For the present, in our country, I venture that the resources of literacy and consciousness (and this is really our hope) are at present reduced to a few pockets of people. . . .A few student groups, a few groups of the poor, a few communities of black people, a few religious groups, a few professionals. These people, one would have to concede, have almost no power. Or more closely regarded, they have drawn away from the illiterate and regressive forms that power has taken. Which is to say, they are learning to read and write. And they are seeking new forms of power. Which is to say, they are learning to read and write. And by the time they have learned to pronounce a few words and understand them, let us say, for instance, the word *man,* by that time they will have found to their unutterable astonishment something that the peasant of Brazil discovered to his: it is possible to be a man.[3]

Perhaps this book will serve as one of the many instruments which will be required before we will be able to unlearn our old and radically deceptive way of speaking. Hopefully it will serve as a primer for achieving a new literacy and advance the possibilities for a genuine public debate on "development."

JAMES LAMB
EXECUTIVE DIRECTOR
CENTER FOR THE STUDY OF DEVELOPMENT AND SOCIAL CHANGE

## notes to "illiteracy in america"

[1]Daniel Berrigan, *No Bars to Manhood* (Doubleday, 1970), pp. 72-75.

[2]See Gunnar Myrdal, *The Challenge of World Poverty* (Pantheon, 1970), pp. 72-75, 275-285.

[3]Berrigan, *op. cit.,* pp. 73-74

# domesticating
# the third world

# by
# Denis Goulet

## introduction

This is the season for development reports. A veritable flood of commissioned studies has rained upon our heads in recent months: the Jackson Report, Pearson Report, Peterson Report, Tinbergen Report, Hannah Report, Rockefeller Report, and innumerable others. It would be wearisome and futile to enumerate them all (cf. Appendix A). But it is pertinent to ask why they were commissioned.

One reason is the desire of aid agencies to evaluate their positions after a first "Development Decade." One detects a new sense of urgency in development circles. As Sir Robert Jackson writes: "Development, it is true, is a long and complex process, but time is not on our side, and it is therefore all the more important to reduce delays to an absolute minimum."[1]
Moreover, development experts are losing confidence in the old formulas of success. In "A Review of Literature on Development Theory"[2] Egbert DeVries concludes that no significant progress in theory has been made in ten years. And Gunnar Myrdal testifies to the bankruptcy of conventional wisdom.[3] Scholars agree with practitioners that development arts are in a state of crisis. Consequently, they are in a receptive mood for new directions. Hence, their eagerness to commission reports.

Two more basic reasons, however, account for this flurry of evaluation. The first is that, notwithstanding all aid efforts, income gaps between rich and poor societies are widening. The second is that support for development aid is flagging, within donor and recipient nations alike. Stewards of aid agencies thus feel a need to develop a new rationale for their function.

Each report, moreover, is the fruit of its own peculiar pressures. Jackson's Report is concerned with coordinating the acephalous United Nations "Machine" and Lester Pearson wishes to prepare the World Bank to play an expanded role in the forthcoming era of greater multilateralism. The Peterson Report tries to provide Richard Nixon with guidelines for United States aid policy while Nelson Rockefeller strives to polish the tarnished image of the United States in Latin America. Finally, Tinbergen's study works to set realistic targets and policies for the United Nation's Second Development Decade. In short, the reports were commissioned because a general sentiment exists that all is not well in the development arena; each document claims to tread new ground, offer "fresh" solutions to old problems, and define viable strategies for the 1970's.

My purpose here is not to present a detailed critique of the reports, taken singly or jointly. Nor is it to catalogue the diagnoses and prescriptions they contain. Rather, it is to offer a view of development which contradicts that implied in most reports. *I have come to conclude that the major recommendations made by the reports are mere palliatives to underdevelopment. The reason is that, upon critical examination, the reports reflect a distorted perspective on development.* This faulty vision constitutes, with exceptions to be noted below, a rationalization for the rich world's desire to domesticate the development of the Third World.

Four questions will be discussed in this essay:

— From which vantage point do the authors of these documents speak?

— Which instruments do they advocate for the domestication of development?

— In illustrative terms, how does the Peterson Report exemplify a policy of mere palliatives?

— What is the response of underdeveloped spokesmen to the analyses and prescriptions contained in the development reports?

**1**

## the vantage point of the reports

Most of the reports listed in Appendix A have been written for agencies representing the "developed" segment of mankind. The notable exception is the statement known as the "Latin American Consensus of Viña del Mar."[4] Nevertheless, the majority of statements mirror the thoughts of those already developed. Upon reading these works, one is struck by the condescending tone: underdevelopment is something which "they" (i.e., other societies) experience, whereas development is something which "we" (the societies for which the authors speak) already possess. Under-development is seen above all as a problem to be solved, not as a scandalous indignity to be abolished. Quite typically the Pearson Report opens with these words:

> On October 27, 1967, in a context of increasing concern about the future of international cooperation for economic development, the then President of the World Bank, Mr. George Woods, suggested a "grand assize" in which an international group of "stature and experience" would "meet together, study the consequences of twenty years of develop-ment assistance, assess the results, clarify the errors and propose the policies which will work better in the future."[5]

Significantly, primary emphasis in discussions is given to *aid* which is but a single facet of the much larger issue, *development.* The text just cited speaks of "development assistance," and Peterson's document stresses even in its title "United States Foreign Assistance." The two United Nations studies (Jackson and Tinbergen), on the other hand, speak explicitly of development, both in the context of the "Second Development Decade." Doubtless it is legitimate for aid donors to assess their policies and performance. But it is no less legitimate for readers to look critically at the manner in which the special vantage point of aid donors colors their conception of the development process. What emerges from such a reading is the suspicion that the interests represented by the authors of the report conflict with those who view development from the vantage point of the receivers, or non-receivers, of aid. Their partial view of development has led the commissioned experts to make three crucial omissions in their reports: socialist models of development are not given serious consideration, no genuine critique of goals is undertaken, and nowhere are the structures of dependence and domination properly analyzed. Such a vantage point is at best unrealistic, at worst hypocritically cynical. But it is the logical outcome of the biases inherent in reports whose special character is to deal with development as something their societies have achieved, whereas others have not. As will appear later in these pages, this is an egregious distortion. But let us now return to the critical omissions.

## socialism omitted

Although socialist development efforts and language elicit great interest in almost all underdeveloped countries, regardless of their own political and economic system, the reports practically ignore this fact. Worse still, notwithstanding declarations about "taking nothing for granted" they in fact take it for granted that development ought to take place within existing world market frameworks. The Pearson Commission, it is true, laments the fact that it has not had any contact with Communist countries. It even voices the diplomatic wish that in the future the cause of development would be better served "if Communist and non-Communist countries could work together more closely in this field."[6] No one can fault the reporters for excluding *information* not available to them. They are to blame, however, for not treating socialism as a significant font of development policy for a large number of underdeveloped nations, including the most populous in the world. This omission reflects the very opposite of the attitude of "taking nothing for granted." Consequently, the critical reader begins to doubt whether the kind of international cooperation for development favored by the reports is not limited to what is compatible with maintaining the privileged position currently enjoyed in the world by market economies.

This omission also biases discussion of the kinds of institutional changes deemed necessary within developing societies. The tacit assumption is simply made that modernization ought not proceed, in prescriptive terms, other than along capitalist lines.[7] Such a procedure eliminates from consideration the need for drastic structural changes within developed societies by assuming that social relations in these societies are basically sound and do not create obstacles to the authentic development of other societies. These are precisely the questions, however, which must not be taken for granted. Two further omissions quite logically flow from this first one, namely: no critique of the basic goals of development is attempted, and a conspicuous silence is kept regarding all phenomena of dependence.

## domesticating the third world

### no critique of goals

The major development reports show much concern with instrumental matters, but far too little with goals. One fatal flaw in this approach is that it eludes normative questions about the good life, good societies, and optimum world order, in the absence of which no sound global directives are possible. One understands of course, that those who are busy doing the urgent things rarely have time for the important things, *viz.* to think out the philosophical implications of their activity. Nevertheless, at a privileged moment of re-assessment, the incapacity of experts to raise the teleological questions posed by development is unpardonable. Some development writers, it is true, (Harbison, Myers, Furtado, Higgins, *et al.*) acknowledge that development is a purely relative accomplishment, itself subordinated to the pursuit of the good life. But most policy planners and scholars have never seriously inquired whether today's alleged development is genuine or spurious. By failing to do so, they feel justified in treating the "underdeveloped" as standing in need of their help. Worse still, their ethnocentrism has prevented them from seeing what is good in "underdeveloped" lands.

This is not to argue that mass poverty is good or that mass affluence is always an evil; nor is it to assume that emotional satisfactions received from primary groups and extended families are necessarily preferable to the anonymity of modern cities. But it is to ask whether the price paid to obtain development's benefits may not often be unnecessarily high;[9] and it is to challenge the primacy accorded economic progress at the expense of more fundamental human values. It is also to suggest, in Erich Fromm's words, that alienation in abundance may be as inimical to human happiness as alienation in misery. *More basically still, it is to question whether present modes of pursuing development do not cripple the ability of most Third World societies to control their own destinies.* Is it to unleash new determinisms upon them without first inquiring into the purely relative character of the benefits gained?

Of equal significance is the complete silence of the reports on the need for austerity within developed countries if the sacrifices demanded of non-developed countries are to be acceptable to them.[10] There is much rhetoric about less developed countries not setting their sights too high lest they be frustrated, i.e., lest the poverty/wealth gap increase. At best the "lucky ones" among Third World countries may reach, by the year 2000, a level of material welfare now enjoyed by West Europeans.[11] Meanwhile the latter will have attained the level of contemporary Americans. And what of Americans? No attempt is made in any of the reports to ask what is consumption for and what is our theory of priority needs. Our authors once again simply assume that mass consumption is a valid good. Moreover, while urging basic changes in consumer patterns upon underdeveloped countries, they are silent about altering those same patterns in their own "developed" countries. Similarly, they make no mention of the enormous waste of resources currently practiced within developed countries, either for the satisfaction of capriciously engineered wants or, more dramatically, for illusory "shibboleth" armament needs. It is worth noting that at a recent conference sponsored by American Quakers[12] (and attended by major contributors to the reports – Sir Robert Jackson, Jan Tinbergen, top staff members from the Pearson and Peterson Reports, World Bank, AID and other representatives), no one seriously discussed the following question placed on the agenda: "To what extent do the various arms races inhibit international development?" Participants tacitly agreed that it was "unrealistic" to discuss this. But is it not even more "unrealistic" to imagine that development is possible for the Third World at large unless developed countries put an end to their monumental waste in producing trivial goods and unless they give up their explosive toys? Quite apart from the massive waste of resources occasioned by the armaments race is the poisoned atmosphere resulting therefrom: any creative steps toward establishing a kind of world order in which development might become possible are thereby precluded.

This is but one of the issues omitted in the reports. The omission is the logical outcome of neglecting to undertake a critique of the goals of development and of treating value questions in a purely instrumental manner.[13]

### structures of dependence

A third omission relegates the issue of dependence to oblivion. For the Pearson Commission, "The major external constraint may be summed up as the availability of foreign exchange."[14] But representatives of twenty-one Latin American nations, on the contrary, propose changes based on principles of cooperation, solidarity, respect for national sovereignty and the people's right to self-determination and on the need for a fairer international division of labour that will favour the rapid economic and social development of the developing countries, instead of impeding it, as has been the case hitherto.[15]

According to them, therefore, the present international division of labour is not equitable and it impedes development in the Third World. They also imply that their peoples' right to self-determination is not being respected by present ground-rules of international "cooperation." Here indeed is the heart of the matter: differential vulnerability in the face of the world's power distribution. What the high-priests of development wisdom are saying is: no power to the poor. Enlightened self-interest leads them to utter lofty pronouncements about "a more equitable sharing among individuals and nations of the benefits of progress."[16] But no shred of evidence exists to show that the demands for autonomy made by underdeveloped nations will be met. Provided low-income societies do not challenge present arrangements governing access to resources, influence, technological invention and an effective voice in world decisions, they will be allowed to get their due share of development's benefits. But development is not reducible to its benefits alone; it is above all a society's capacity to master its own historical destiny. Economically, there is a world of difference between economic progress and the progressivity of the economy. On the broader development front, it is the difference between being the agent of one's development as defined in one's own terms, and being a mere beneficiary of development as defined by someone else.

None of the reports mentions the lasting effects of economic or political domination, of differential bargaining strength among putative "partners" to development transfers. At this point the omission of socialist development models, mentioned above, assumes new proportions. If one chooses to exclude socialist countries in his survey of development efforts, he is led to point to Korea, Taiwan or Greece as examples of encouraging growth rates. Yet each of these countries has had to pay the very high price of subservience to American policy in exchange for substantial aid. And no major changes have taken place in their domestic social structures, which remain archaic and paternalistic. Can one seriously consider development to have taken place, therefore, merely because aggregate production has risen? Is not China's achievement a much truer index of "development": the abolition of mass starvation, the destruction of inequitable land tenure practices, the universalization of education? Likewise, Cuba's achievement in emancipating itself from undue dependence on an alien economy and in radically reconstructing its domestic society may stand as a more basic index of development than rises in GNP or industrial investment. What seems to be at issue, ultimately, is one's view of what underdevelopment is.

For developed capitalist societies, and for those institutions which do not fundamentally challenge those societies, underdevelopment is basically a lack and a lag. It is a *lack* of those technological, economic, administrative, and cultural conditions which assure certain kinds of performance. Concurrently it is a *lag* or backwardness, as compared to societies presently out front, in achieving that same performance. Given this view of things, it is logical to portray the development process as an exercise in problem-solving: the task is to mobilize and allocate resources rationally, and to introduce behavior and institutions which foster "modernity." But a society can achieve all this while still remaining subservient to others which have arrived before it on history's development scene.

If, conversely, one considers underdevelopment as the by-product of development itself,[17] he understands that differential structures of vulnerability – economic, political and cultural – simultaneously explain both underdevelopment and the difficulty of overcoming it. Underdeveloped nations must conquer dignity in the very struggle they wage to gain their bread. But dignity can never be won if a society is perpetually kept in a state of historical adolescence. This is precisely what mainland China has so well understood: that there is something distressingly ethnocentric in the analysis of the problem in terms of development and underdevelopment. Above all else, the central question is a people's historical consciousness as prelude to its historical agency in framing its own progress.

To postulate structural vulnerability as the key to understanding underdevelopment and fostering development is not to fall into any simplistic "scapegoat" theory of history. This needs to be made clear because Western scholars tend to assume that any analysis of economic imperialism or neocolonialism constitutes an atavistic regression to primitive nineteenth century Marxism or to credulity in a form of propaganda now rendered obsolete by the accession of African and Asian ex-colonies to political independence. This, however, is not the case, for underdevelopment is not primarily non-development or a low level of living but a special kind of total trauma which results from dependence.

The trauma is total because the desire mechanisms of an entire populace are altered before it possesses control over the social institutions which would enable it to gain effective use of resources needed to meet these new desires. Those who do possess the resources or enjoy access to them understandably "assist" the development effort of others only to the degree that such activity enhances their own objectives. Since they are technologically and economically more powerful, transfers of resources, information and personnel consolidate the dominant position of the strong and further accentuate the dependence of the weak.

To omit such considerations in any overall assessment of development is to distort reality in serious fashion. Sociologists of knowledge repeatedly warn us that any group's interests color its perceptions of reality. Societies and classes already developed have a vested interest in portraying the development process as they do; their mastery over historical change processes would be undermined were they to do otherwise. Nevertheless, growing numbers of critical spokesmen in underdeveloped countries are piercing through this veil of mystification. Later in this essay I shall discuss the refusal of the Third World to be domesticated. At this juncture it suffices to call attention to the serious omission in the report. This defect helps explain the view which the stewards of development entertain of "partnership."

### partnership among unequals

Although it is titled *Partners in Development,* the Pearson Report speaks pessimistically of the "aid relationship" through which this partnership has presumably been established.

> It is not only among the developed countries that the climate has deteriorated. On the developing side too there are signs of frustration and impatience. In much of the developing world there is a sense of disillusion about the very nature of the aid relationship.[18]

Later we are told that

> Both sides have learned that cooperation for development means more than a simple transfer of funds. It means a set of new relationships which must be founded on mutual understanding and self-respect . . . .Wealth does not entitle a rich and powerful country to dominate another country's national life as a consequence of the aid it may have given . . . . The "development relationship," which is at the heart of efficient aid policy, must be based on a clear division of responsibilities which meets the needs of both partners.[19]

This high sounding language, however, masks what economist Michael Hudson calls development as "a game of partners and pawns." The tenure of the Report, he says, is to encourage the Bank "to continue financing poverty rather than the struggles out of poverty."[20] The fallacy of the Commissioners consists in assuming that development will meet the needs of both partners. To use the words of the Pearson Report, "Development assistance differs from other forms of aid in that it ought to be directed to a clear objective which joins donor and recipient in a finite enterprise beneficial to both."[21] Nothing is further from the truth, since under present exchange arrangements mutual benefit is often precluded. The development needs enunciated by Third World spokesmen in the "Charter of Algiers," at UNCTAD II, or in "The Latin American Consensus of Viña del Mar" are not compatible with the image "developed" countries have of their own needs. The reporters say we live in a "village world" or international community. What they fail to add is that "elders" rule over this village world and that *they* are the "elders." As a result, the portrait of development painted by spokesmen for aid agencies negates the Third World's quest for autonomy and for control over technological change. Therefore, the language of partnership employed by the stronger partner in the dialogue is sheer mystification, because there can be no valid partnership without reciprocity. And reciprocity can only be established if the stronger partners are themselves made vulnerable in their relationships with weaker partners.

Here is one example of how the thinking of donor groups is vitiated in questions dealing with reciprocity:

During the summer of 1968 the Center for International Studies of the Massachusetts Institute of Technology sponsored, jointly with the U.S. Agency for International Development, a six-week summer study on Title IX of the Foreign Assistance Act of 1966. This Title calls upon the Agency for International Development to emphasize "Assuring maximum participation in the task of economic development on the part of the people of the developing countries, through the encouragement of democratic private and local governmental institutions." In the course of their debates, the assembled experts faced the question whether the United States can suitably provide technical assistance to underdeveloped countries in the area of urban problems. This is obviously one problem Americans have not known how to solve at home. One may legitimately ask, therefore, if U.S. urbanists have any counsels of value to offer their counterparts in poorer lands. After overcoming the debilitating effects of its own humility, the seminar group replied as follows:

> The fact that the U.S. has been unable to resolve its own city problems should not lead Americans to stay out of this area in the Third World. Quite the contrary, for it offers a unique opportunity. In most fields of endeavour, the undoubted technological superiority of Americans has a stifling and discouraging effect on their host country counterparts. In the area of urban problems, however, we have a rare chance to share ideas and information on a basis of equality.[22]

What is disconcerting is that these experts fail to perceive that the stifling effect produced on hosts by the "undoubted technological superiority of Americans" needs to be offset in every technical transfer, not just in the special case of urban expertise. Technical superiority in all cases needs to be seen as a purely relative accomplishment implying no valid claim to superiority. Not only technology but development itself is simply an instrumental goal subordinated to broader human goods. Once they recognize this, development agents lose their illusion of superiority over the recipients of their advice. But if superior political and economic strength is viewed as an index of absolute superiority, experts will continue to display a patronizing spirit in their relations with others. What needs to be overturned is their very conception of what development is. To paraphrase Keynes, economic development is merely the possibility of development.

Institutional vulnerability of their own is needed to force technical experts to practice reciprocity with counterparts.[23] Inequalities in technical transfers are only part of the problem, however. Certain more basic disparities in the respective bargaining positions of developed and underdeveloped nations are operative in multilateral and international organizations. To illustrate, the World Bank with its affiliates accounted for nearly 60% of gross disbursements of multilateral agencies in 1967.[24] Since most of the Bank's funds come from a few industrialized countries, "it appears, in the eyes of some of its clients in the developing world, as uncomfortably linked to the big and wealthy powers."[25] Voting rights are weighted in favor of major contributors: low-income countries have only 35% of the votes in World Bank and affiliated organizations.[26]

Under such structural arrangements, there is no substance behind the rhetoric of partnership: reciprocal bargaining strength is lacking. One is reminded of the language used by government officials within the United States as they fervently call upon this nation's Black population to join hands with them and solve common problems together. At present levels of critical awareness, most Black leaders correctly interpret the invitation as a device used by their antagonists for not coming to grips with real complaints. Unfortunately, it is likewise in the development debate. Those already developed quite obviously have a vested interest in suggesting a partnership based on the imagery of smooth, harmonious collaboration. The victims of inequality, on the other hand, know that development processes are unavoidably conflictual, disequilibrating, often traumatic. They also understand that genuine partnership is possible only after their own structural vulnerability has been overcome. Only then can they begin to speak to their interlocutors with reciprocal strength and influence. The form of partnership proposed to them in the development reports is a sham, and they know it.

# II

## the instruments of domestication

To "domesticate," in common parlance, means to tame a wild animal so as to render it harmless for life in a household. Used metaphorically, the term aptly describes how groups and societies already developed seek to channel the savage forces unleashed by development so as not to upset their own positions of privilege. One cannot doubt that the representatives of developed societies are fully aware of the seething resentment harbored by their underdeveloped counterparts. As early as 1957 Myrdal could write that the peoples in underdeveloped countries and their spokesmen

> show an inclination to put part of the blame for their poverty on the rest of the world and, in particular, on the countries which are better off—or, rather they attribute the inequalities to the world economic system which keeps them so poor while other nations are so rich and becoming richer.[27]

Even "moderate" leaders in underdeveloped countries do not want their societies to become mere cultural or political satellites of the world's developed metropoles. The permanent prospect of never "catching up" with the rich world is galling to them. Equally humiliating is the likelihood of never achieving technological autonomy or an effective voice in international decision making.

Development's benefits can be won of course in various ways: through capitalistic enterprise, socialist planning, mixed economy patterns, dynamic communitarian structures, and so on. Notwithstanding this plurality of models, however, the authors of the development reports under discussion seem to exclude all patterns of development which threaten the dominant role presently enjoyed by the developed countries and interest groups. As Ivan Illich writes:

> There is a normal course for those who make development policies, whether they live in North or South America, in Russia or Israel. *It is to define development and to set its goals in ways with which they are familiar, which they are accustomed to use in order to satisfy their own needs, and which permit them to work through the institutions over which they have power or control.* This formula has failed, and must fail. There is not enough money in the world for development to succeed along these lines, not even in the combined arms and space budgets of the super-powers.[28]

The "haves" of the world wish to domesticate the development of the "have-nots" because they fear such things as the assertive national pride of mainland China as a model for imitation, or the drastic social reconversion effectuated domestically by the government of Cuba. Under the guise of advocating a non-ideological path to development, the rich now preach the merits of two choice instruments of domestication: multilateral aid and multinational corporations.

## multilateral aid

Although bilateral transfers still account for almost 90% of total development aid, the pendulum has now begun to swing in the opposite direction. All reports advocate increasing aid's multilateral component. The evils of bilateralism are too obvious: discriminatory selection of recipients for reasons unrelated to development needs or performance, the appearance (and reality) of charity and interventionism, the spreading of aid too thinly to cover large numbers of projects and programs. The main objection, however, is that bilateral aid reinforces the dominant position enjoyed by donors over recipients. Greater awareness of this drawback has quite understandably led even major bilateral donors, including the United States,[29] to resort to the glowing language of multilateralism. In conferences and official documents, spokesmen from underdeveloped countries are repeatedly told that all these drawbacks will be removed, that a truly international effort on the basis of need and performance will characterize future transfers. This argument is misleading, however, in two respects.

The first is that the contemplated shifts to multilateralism are extremely modest. Pearson, for instance, recommends merely that

> *aid-providers increase grants and capital subscriptions for multilateral development aid programs to a minimum of 20 percent of the total flow of official development assistance by 1975.*[30]

The report drafted by the Committee for Economic Development mentions no specific percentage but merely advocates.

> *a gradual transition to a larger use of multilateral aid by channelling additions to U.S. development lending through international institutions as they acquire the capability to administer the additional resources and as other aid donors are prepared to increase their contributions.*[31]

Nevertheless, the Committee stresses private investments and other flows to such an extent that one suspects it is thinking of a modest switch to multilateralism largely to "get the political heat off the

U.S." In short, even the heralded new trend to multilateralism will not greatly reduce the predominant role played by bilateral aid. Moreover, much of the "multilateral" aid projected in the future is simply a form of disguised bilateral transfer, renamed in order to minimize the unpleasant connotations attaching to massive intervention in recipient countries.

The second, more basic, objection to multilateralism as presently conceived is that it does not reduce the dependence of Third World nations one iota. As one Asian ambassador recently told me, it is as humiliating for his country to be a satellite of the World Bank as of the United States. Furthermore, many supposedly multi-lateral organizations are effectively controlled by the chief bilateral donors and serve largely as "fronts" for precisely those interests to which poor recipients are most vulnerable: powerful governments from developed countries, business and technical interests from these same countries, and trans-national bureaucracies. Consequently, to switch to multilateralism may simply be a device used by developed countries, fearful of the greater awareness on the part of poorer ones of the price they pay for aid, for "getting the monkey off their back." Indeed, one South American ambassador recently declared, at the Quaker Conference mentioned earlier, that it may be better for his country to keep dealing with bilateral donors. In these cases, at least, it has a bit of political leverage in bargaining. But with the International Monetary Fund, the World Bank, IDA, it has none at all!

One must not suppose of course that all multilateral aid is equally acceptable or repugnant to recipients. United Nations organizations, whatever be their operational weaknesses—and Sir Robert Jackson in his Report has pointed to them with clarity and courage—are probably the least "tainted" of the donors. On the other hand the Pearson, Peterson, CED and similar reports glibly assume that the World Bank and other agencies are genuine international organizations which operate above the "political and commercial interests" of mere nation states. Third World leaders know that this is clearly not the case. They already suspect the mystification which lies behind the new language of multi-lateralism; indeed they recognize that language as a novel instrument of domestication.

## multinational corporations

One notes throughout the reports a recurring theme: the beneficence of multinational corporations. The arguments advanced in

27

favor of such entities [32] appear to have been uncritically endorsed by the authors of the reports. The case for multinational corporations rests on the claims that:

— private investment is one form of genuine development aid;

— trans-national corporations do not serve the interests of national groups, but those of the international community;

— they bargain on a basis of partnership with host countries or organizations: namely, that mutual interests bring them together in an equitable contractual arrangement;

— they are in the vanguard of technological and managerial expertise, which they are willing to transfer generously to the Third World in exchange for "reasonable" profits;

— their net effect is to render the private sector dynamic through the increase in jobs, heightened productivity and efficiency, the training of indigenous personnel, linkage effects with other units of production (of goods and services), and the like.

The central point at issue, however, is not whether multinational corporations serve the national interests of some countries. In my judgment, with each passing year the very opposite is true: nations themselves are made to serve the interests of an international techno-structure. The crucial question is this: Does the multinational corporation, ruled by a technostructure with international ambitions, make a major contribution to authentic development? There is no doubt that it is efficient and productive and that it can even provide "social" benefits for its servants. But does it not stifle the aspirations after relative autonomy which are a necessary ingredient of development? The presence of large multinational corporations inevitably has profound effects on social stratification in the direction of an ever more elitist pattern of social control. Here as before the instrument favored prejudges the case against precisely the kinds of efforts realized in socialist (China, Cuba) or communitarian (Tanzania) development models. It completely short-circuits questions of cultural and political independence and of social stratification. It is, in a word, a marvelous instrument of domestication. As long as the Third World develops in a manner which will create a safe climate–and, be it added, generous profits–for the multinational corporations, then all the developed countries' resources are available for well-behaved low-income groups. If, however, they wish to develop without becoming subservient to gigantic, elitist, technocratic enterprises, then the stewards of massive resources will go elsewhere.

Galbraith has explained (in *The Industrial State*) how the United States' domestic technostructure has learned to subordinate its thirst for profits to the needs of survival and of power consolidation. International technostructures are quickly learning the same lesson. They are, however, as powerless to solve the problems of underdevelopment in the Third World at large as United States private enterprise is to bring salvation to our city ghettoes and depressed areas. The very logic of optimum-profits in a managed competitive framework is incompatible with the demands of underdeveloped sectors and areas. This is true quite apart from the claim that private enterprise is more efficient than public counterparts.[33]

Here, too, as in the question of multilateralism versus bilateralism, it is no better for politics and economics to be beholden to international technostructures than to industrialized nation-states. The international ambitions of nations are, in plain fact, to a large degree expressed by the expansionism of multinational corporations. At best, multinational corporations, if stringently disciplined, may make a modest contribution to industrialization and the modernization of services. But this is possible only on condition that their scope of action is strictly limited. As we shall argue later, profound and basic changes in world economic structures are necessary before genuine development can become possible for the world at large. Moreover, as the Viña del Mar document asserts, it is illusory to continue regarding investments made by private firms as a form of development aid. In the view of the twenty-one Latin American signatories, it is necessary

> To agree that private foreign investment should not be considered as aid or calculated as part of financial cooperation for development purposes. Foreign private investment, subject to national decisions and priorities, should try to promote the mobilization of internal resources, create income and prevent outflows of foreign technological contribution, and act as a complementary factor in national investment preferably in association with it. This has not always been so in the past.[34]

Nor does it promise to be so in the future if the uncritical advocacy of multi national corporationism found in the reports goes unchecked. Even in the best of circumstances such corporations can only be "a complementary factor in national investment, preferably in association with it."

It may well be that, given present levels of experience in underdeveloped lands with foreign investors, future conditions of equity will require a number of disciplinary measures. These might include insistence on indigenous voting control (therefore, only minority stockholding by foreigners), a tax on repatriated profits (over and above the ordinary profit taxes), a limited time-period after which foreign ownership (even if it is only partial) would revert to the hands of citizens from the host countries. Perhaps the most controversial clause might be the requirement that no investment guarantees be offered by powerful patron governments or international banking agencies. This stipulation manifestly violates all conventional wisdom on this question. Nevertheless, from the vantage point of the vulnerable host country, the kind of private investment that would refuse this discipline risks not being equitable.

Such disciplinary measures appear reasonable to guarantee autonomy in underdeveloped countries, but they obviously appear unreasonable to investors. That they should so appear is one indication that the logic of the international technostructure leads it to expand its own power and profits, not to contribute to the autonomous development of the "international community." An analysis like the one just sketched out has the merit, if no other, of revealing how the multinational corporation, as presently championed by spokesmen from developed countries and interest groups, is an instrument of domestication of Third World development. The reports constantly beg the question by referring to a "dynamic private sector." They fail to ask whether a sector is dynamic precisely *qua* private and, more importantly, they make no attempt to analyze the domination effects which can be exercised even by a dynamic sector. Dominance and dependence are simply excluded from their examination of the development equation.

The technological supremacy enjoyed by interest groups already developed (whether nations, multinational corporate groups or international technocrats) is protected by the formula of "development via multilateral aid plus multinational corporate investment." Inasmuch as the capacity to sustain technological innovation is the most decisive resource and capital factor over the long-term, the condition of technological dependence which presently characterizes the Third World is a necessary by-product of the recommendations urged by the reports under discussion. To the extent, therefore, that indigenous technological mastery is an element of authentic development, it follows that those recommendations are at best mere palliatives to underdevelopment.

# III
## the peterson report
## the rationale for domestication

On March 4, 1970 a Task Force on International Development delivered its Report to the President entitled "U.S Foreign Assistance in the 1970's: A New Approach." More than all others this report exemplifies the rationalization by a group of experts of the intent of the United States not to promote but to "domesticate" development. The mandate given to the task force, headed by Rudolph A. Peterson, President of the Bank of America, was to examine United States foreign economic and military assistance programs, our trade and investment relations with the developing countries, and the fundamental problems that the United States faces in this area of foreign policy. Members were instructed "to take nothing for granted" while recommending "policies that will serve the best interests of our Nation." This is already to take for granted, however, that the best interest of our Nation are always compatible with the demands of development in the rest of the world. I have discussed elsewhere[35] the contradictions which exist between the professed goals of the Alliance for Progress and the geopolitical considerations which, in reality, determine the United States' stance *vis-a-vis* its Latin American "partners" in that alliance. To speak bluntly, the national interests of this country, as presently defined by our leaders, are hostile to the cause of authentic development in the Third World. It is precisely this contradiction which the Peterson group fails to scrutinize.

The United States is urged to continue being selective in distributing its aid. The proposed International Development Bank, Peterson tells us, "would enable the United States to continue to take up its share, with other nations, of programs in India, Pakistan, Indonesia, and selected African countries and to support Latin America development, which is of special concern to the United States" (p. 26). A deadening "spheres of influence" imagery hovers over countless other assertions. Behind it all is the old specter of the Cold War. The persistence of such imagery is what robs the Peterson Report of any credibility: a "new approach" is promised, but all we get is the illusion of re-appraisal. Perhaps the only novelty is greater sophistication in disguising the traditional foreign policy objectives of the United States behind the language of "international" institutions: development banks, development institutes, development councils. Quite significantly, however, each of the "international" institutions is thoroughly

Americanized. Thus, President Nixon is urged to restructure this nation's foreign aid machinery around four administrative components: a U. S. International Development Bank, a U. S. International Development Institute, a U. S. International Development Council, and an Overseas Private Investment Corporation. These recommendations constitute, at best, minor tinkering with the present system. There is no evidence to show that this nation's development experts are prepared to give serious attention to the complaints voiced at Viña del Mar or at the latest UNCTAD conference. To illustrate, the Viña del Mar document speaks with concern of the scientific and technological gap which continues to grow between the United States and Latin America, of structural problems flowing from the workings of the international monetary system, of conditions of maritime transport which hinder and add to the cost of Latin America's foreign trade, of the increasing burden of debt servicing, and so on. None of these is treated adequately by the Peterson Report. One is forced to conclude, therefore, that its authors clearly intend, not to abolish domestication of the Third World by the United States, but merely to disguise it.

The demand by Latin American countries that private foreign investment no longer be treated as "aid" is completely ignored. Instead the Peterson document blandly declares that "U.S. international development policies should seek to widen the use of private initiative, private skills, and private resources in the developing countries" (p. 30).

More shocking is the discredited practice of labelling military transfers as "assistance." Such language informs the reader that no lessons have been learned by this country's leaders in the last decade. We are expected to believe that

> Security assistance is an essential tool of U.S. foreign policy. Its goals are: to improve the military defenses of our allies and move them toward greater military self-reliance, to serve as a substitute for the deployment of U.S. forces abroad, to pay for U.S. base rights, and to deal with crisis situations. The size and specific objectives of these programs are subject to reassessment at any time. Their relation to national interests, however, is straightforward: they use resources for purposes essential to U.S. security. (p. 6)

The patronizing unrealism of the report is at least consistent: it reappears throughout. Thus, much is made of the barriers to development found in developing countries themselves: "Unresponsive social and political systems, severe deficiencies of technical skills, and others." But not a single word about the barriers to Third World development posed by the United States: its disproportionate use of the world's resources for largely wasteful and warlike production, its alliances, overt and covert, with governments which veto domestic structural reforms, its "selective" aid to those nations which provide a "safe" climate for foreign investment and United States political interests. The dominant philosophy behind the report seems to be that which characterized free-booting entrepreneurs last century: "the poor are miserable because they are unimaginative and lazy. If they show a little goodwill and work hard, we will help them climb the ladder of success (what remains unsaid, of course, is the proviso 'up to a certain level')." This "hidden ceiling" on modernization underlying United States thinking is unmasked, however, in such sanctimonious declarations as the following: "it is U.S. policy to discourage developing countries from obtaining sophisticated military equipment" (p.14). Is this in order to assure the United States an unencumbered market on which to sell its surplus scrap weapons? High moral principles are repeatedly invoked to justify an "altruistic" development policy. By a felicitious coincidence, however, this is done only in cases where United States interests are enhanced by the altruism. Whenever "moral" principles could be adduced by representatives of low-income countries, in opposition to United States policy, Mr. Peterson and his colleagues (the Task Force comprises seven businessmen or bankers, five academics or foundation personnel, two lawyers, one general and one cardinal) grow mysteriously silent. By appealing to a "realistic" form of prudence, they declare themselves ready to sacrifice illusory large gains in favor of more modest but "attainable" goals.

The Overseas Development Council has appraised the probable reception of the Peterson Report by the American public as follows. In its press release of March 13, 1970, the Council states:

> To those already convinced of the potential value of overseas development assistance and the need for a changed approach in its broad outline for the 1970's, the Peterson Task Force Report is an encouraging, thoroughly modern document. To those undecided about the U.S. role in the world, and to those skeptical about the value of U.S. foreign assistance even if well managed, the report will be less persuasive.

Such language is misleading. Many American students of development are convinced of the potential value of overseas development assistance and of the need for a changed approach. Nevertheless, they judge that it is not simply a matter of improving the administration or management of United States assistance, but of modifying the ground rules which govern this country's relationships with undeveloped countries. This view imposes on the United States painful domestic changes as well as changes in its foreign policy. More will be said about these changes in later pages.

It would be monotonous to pass in review all the stated and unstated premises which go to buttress the cumulative wisdom of Peterson's experts on development. A single, but revealing, indication of the self-righteous obtuseness which permeates the document, however, is the matter-of-fact inclusion of United States war expenses in Vietnam as part of the nation's "foreign assistance" (p. 38). In the very next paragraph, however, as the authors of the report launch into their peroration, they inform Mr. Nixon that with their approach

> The Task Force believes that this country can take up the challenge of international development in a way that adds a new dimension to U.S. foreign policy and creates a broad and hopeful vision of the world and its future. Americans, young and old, can then take renewed pride in playing a constructive world role and in meeting the obligations of global citizenship.

There is very little to Peterson's report in which any American who is freed from ethnocentric United States mythology can take pride. To lay bare the full panoply of the experts' collective unwisdom would be tedious; a brief word regarding the four new institutions recommended will suffice.

The President, it will be recalled, is urged to create a U.S. International Bank, a U.S. International Institute, a U. S. International Council, and an Overseas Private Investment Corporation. The overt aim is to shift from a bilateral to a multilateral framework for dispensing aid. In the words of the report, "A predominantly bilateral U. S. program is no longer politically tenable in our relations with many developing countries, nor is it advisable in view of what other countries are doing in international development" (p.22). Operations of the world financing system will need to be expanded. This system includes the World Bank and its affiliates, the International Development Association, the International Monetary Fund, the United Nations Development Program, and a number of regional development banks. Financial assistance levels envisaged are as follows: in addition to an aggregate, multi-year appropriation of $5 billion to set up the International Development Bank and International Development Institute, Peterson recommends that United States contributions to international agencies be increased by $500 million so as to reach, by 1972, an annual total level of $1.1 billion. He further suggests that $300 million, to be obtained from principal and interest payments on loans presently outstanding, be made available to the bank. Moreover, food programs should continue at the level of $1 billion yearly.

What is sought in all this is a strengthened international operation which "would set the framework for the bilateral assistance programs of the United States and other industrialized countries" (p.23). Under this general system

> international agencies would assume primary responsibility for analyzing conditions and policies in developing countries, for establishing close working relations with appropriate officials in these countries, and for determining total capital and technical assistance requirements and the policies necessary for effective use of investment resources. (p. 23)

Nothing is said, however, about modifying the distribution of control within this network, now to be more closely interlocking, of allegedly "international" organizations. That they are international in their membership and in the locus of their operations is certainly true. On the other hand, that they are authentically international in their decision-making apparatus and their ideological content remains doubtful. One suspects that the Peterson Commission has very well understood that powerful industrialized nation-states can neutralize much of the opposition to their policies of domination by transferring the onus to an embryonic alliance between trans-national public and multi national private institutions, both of which have vested interests in the same mode of development as the developed capitalist countries. They also know of course that industrialized socialist countries can very comfortably live with such an alliance. Therefore, at least the appearances of ideological collaboration can be maintained.

It does not seem amiss to conclude that the array of new institutions imagined by the commission is mainly a device to get United States bilateral machinery "in tune" with the "wave of the future": an unchallengeable consortium of trans-national elitist technocrats, public and private. The "new" multilateral organizations, however, are mere palliatives, similar in conception to the CIAP (Interamerican Committee for the Alliance for Progress) created in São Paulo in November, 1963, to give Latin American critics of United States bilateralism the illusion of redress of grievances. Viewed in this perspective, no matter how sweeping the institutional changes recommended by Peterson appear on the surface, they remain insignificant. A further word regarding the Overseas Private Investment Council (OPIC) illustrates to what degree the crucial omissions mentioned earlier distort the development problem.

## overseas private investment council

With delicate and tender anguish over the "misunderstandings" which have conferred upon foreign private investment such a bad (and undeserved?) reputation, the report discusses "private incentives and market forces" (pp. 18 ff.). We are told that rapid economic progress usually takes place where "a favorable environment for private initiative" exists. Moreover, "if the goal is economic development, the issue is one of efficiency, not ideology" (p. 18). This is a surprising declaration, inasmuch as the report declares that development is something far more complex and comprehensive than mere economic progress. On page 27 we read:

> In making loans for development purposes, the United States should recognize that development is more than an economic process. It should take into account not only the extent to which a loan will contribute to economic growth but also the extent to which it will encourage social and civic development and will result in a wide dispersion of benefits.

Apparently this piece of salutary wisdom is not meant to apply in the case of private investment. Here the issue is simply efficiency, not ideology or broader social goals!

Even regarding efficiency, however, the point is debatable. Seymour Melman's studies[36] suggest that higher efficiency does not necessarily correlate with private ownership or management. Efficiency is surely important, but not efficiency at any cost or efficiency of any sort whatsoever. And it is precisely here that ideology steps in: to define the priority of social objectives, as well as to determine which social costs are tolerable and which are not. In their treatment of private incentives and market forces, Peterson's reporters never mention the broader social and civic goals of development. It is as though they had never heard of the distinction long ago established by Mannheim[37] between competitive free enterprise as an organizing principle of an economy and the same institution as a social mechanism for regulating efficiency. Consequently, their plea for efficiency is itself a value-laden, ideological defense of a partisan position. This is legitimate, of course, but it is better done overtly. In truth, private enterprise can play, under the properly disciplined conditions outlined above, a useful subordinate role in development. Yet it is strange to note that the Peterson team, so conversant with the best of American thought, seems totally oblivious to a major point made by Professor Neil Jacoby, a leading expert on the multinational corporation and himself a vigorous champion of private overseas investment.

As he discusses joint ventures in socialist countries, there designated as "industrial cooperation," Jacoby comments that arrangements reached seem to produce a situation in which "there is no basis for feelings of 'exploitation' of one country by the others."[38] Briefly, these arrangements are as follows:

— The foreign private investors enter into collaboration with a public firm in the host country. The crux here, I maintain, is not that the partner is a public entity, but that it is not unduly vulnerable to a more powerful partner.

— The private investor supplies technical and managerial services, but the host counterpart produces and markets. This division of labor is obviously calculated to keep the foreign influence within manageable bounds..

— The foreign company shares in the profits from sales and is paid a fee for its technical and managerial services.

— In Jacoby's words,

> Socialist ideology, which precludes private ownership of fixed capital, has caused East-West industrial cooperation to take place on a basis of loans rather than equity capital. Yet cracks have appeared in this ideological barrier. The Foreign Investment Law of Yugoslavia was ammended during 1967 to permit joint ventures of Yugoslavian and foreign companies to acquire ownership of domestic fixed assets.[39]

At a recent seminar, the possibility that Yugoslavia might eventually allow foreign firms to own equity capital was evoked. Participants judged, moreover, "that the fifty-fifty investment division could be accepted if the Yugoslav partner thought that this was advantageous for him. All provisions of the model appeared to be easily acceptable under Yugoslav law."[40]

Jacoby believes that the penetration of European and Japanese business into socialist nations of Eastern Europe in novel ways may have "effects that may ultimately be even more momentous for the world than their operations within market economies." I fully agree. One major difficulty perdures, however: the paradigmatic values of this penetration for cases where the foreign investment takes place in non-socialist countries is not perceived. Yet, what appears of central importance is that the partnership is not allowed to place the host country in a position of vulnerability. Hence, the emphasis on loans, profit-sharing, fee-paying for technological services, etc.... As compared with these developments, the recommendations of the Peterson report are stale and unimaginative. They seem rather to have been designed to overcome the "bad image" of private foreign investment, not to attenuate its domination effects.

One final point on private overseas investment is worthy of attention: insurance guarantees. Peterson urges OPIC to

> make greater use of the U.S. guaranty programs, in combination with those of other countries, to encourage international joint ventures. These multinational projects, open to investors in the host countries, help to reduce nationalist sensitivities to foreign investment." (p. 22)

The crucial point, however, is not to reduce national sensitivities to foreign investment, but to lessen the vulnerability of host-country enterprises *vis-a-vis* foreign investment units. Even assuming a joint venture between two private firms, one domestic, the other foreign, there is no valid reason why the foreign firm should be insured against nationalizations, acts-of-God, and other untoward acts, whereas its domestic partner, often more vulnerable initially, should not enjoy similar protection. If equity is what is sought, both partners ought to enjoy identical guarantees. On this question the Peterson report, as it so often does, simply takes prevailing assumptions for granted and suggests nothing new. It is always argued that the "image" of United States operations in the developed world is deficient. Never does Peterson consider, even remotely, the possibility that the "substance" is at fault. Therefore, OPIC is a great idea – for United States businessmen! For the Third World at large, it is something less than a great idea.

In conclusion, the Peterson report breaks no new ground on fundamental issues: United States ethnocentrism, the distorting effects of United States foreign policy caused by this nation's definition of its national security needs and world interests, its uncritical belief in the soundness of its particular arrangements for assuring resource use throughout the world, and the assumption that political stability is to be safeguarded, although we are told that development implies change which is often disruptive (p. 2).

Within the limits of the old conventional wisdom on foreign aid, the Peterson recommendations represent a new approach. Judged according to basic structural needs of the world at large, however, they offer mere palliatives and repeat old blunders. This is not to

**domesticating the third world**

say that the document has no value: but it is to say that its values serve those who already enjoy development's benefits. It stands as a pure Weberian case of the effort by the rich to domesticate the development of the poor.

# IV
## the historic refusal
## no more domestication

New expectations aroused by the development "myth" are not confined to material benefits; they also extend to a search for cultural dignity. Under the stimulus of the multiple social forces impinging upon them, individuals and communities heretofore passive and uncritical grow alert to new meanings in their personal and collective lives. There gradually emerges among them a new and explicit consciousness of themselves, of their present condition, of change processes which hold out hope to them, and of improved conditions to which they might tend as toward some goal. A major element in this emerging consciousness is a desire for recognition or esteem. I cannot here discuss the full range of this desire and the diverse conditions of its genesis in preconscious populations.[41] Rather, I shall confine myself here to describing the altered perceptions in non-developed groups regarding their relations with "developed" counterparts. My argument is that a diffuse but nonetheless identifiable political will is in the process of formation throughout the underdeveloped world, whose objective is to resist those social forces and agents which seek to domesticate their development efforts. My discussion centers on two issues: (1) emerging consciousness itself; (2) Third World analyses of development and suitable change strategies.

## 1. emerging consciousness of the third world

Political dependence is such an overt form of subordination that the drive to abolish colonialism understandably served as precursor to an explicit awareness of other, more subtle, forms of dependence. This is one reason why such terms as "economic imperialism," "neo-colonialisms," "cultural imperialisms" and the like have found ready acceptance in the vocabulary of spokesmen from non-developed groups. It was but a small step to extend the concept of a metropole dominating a satellite to the domestic stratification within poorer countries themselves, even after political independence had been won. Thus one reads of "internal colonialism" practiced by one region, tribe or economic sector in a country at the expense of some other.[42] For sophisticated intellectuals in former colonies, it was not difficult to detect analogies between the kind of exchanges (in goods, capital, personnel and services) which prevailed in colonial times and those characterizing their societies after independence. In both cases, a small group of privileged elite, indifferent to the needs of the population at large, controlled most decisions affecting such exchanges and enjoyed the lion's share of the benefits accruing therefrom. Once this was clearly perceived, it became common to view one's state of "underdevelopment" itself as a by-product of the development of others. Otherwise stated, although it was true that underdevelopment was both a "lack" and a "lag" – the absence of modern technical and economic levels of performance as well as retardation in comparison with other societies – this was not the whole story, nor even its most important element. What became increasingly apparent was that underdevelopment is also, and primarily, a condition of dependence and disjointedness.[43] Dependence has replaced subsistence autarchy or primitive commercial circuits marked by a high degree of reciprocity. And disjointedness had resulted from the implantation of a modern sector serving exogenous interests in the midst of a larger matrix unstructured to enjoy its spread or "trickle-down" benefits. Thus a sharp distinction could be made between the *benefits* of development, and *control* over the processes of development. In the colonial situation, it was obvious that the major portion of the benefits went to the foreign masters. Nevertheless, some benefits were likewise distributed to native upper classes who chose to collaborate, actively or passively, with the designs of the colonizers. Active collaborators included bureaucrats and government officials, professional men, technicians, overseers, merchants and others. Passive collaborators included landowners who agreed with a scheme of land use favoring export crops at the expense of food grown for local use, or who adjusted their practices to profit from the dislocations provoked by the foreign intrusion. Nevertheless, even those native groups which shared in development's benefits gained little or no control over the processes by which those benefits were generated. Control and decision-making were denied them.

Since they already enjoyed some share of material benefits, however, and since they had received the education of the colonizers, they quite predictably began to make demands for political independence. Anti-colonial independence movements were, accordingly, largely staffed by native elite or middle groups (labor leaders, civil servants, and the like). So as to win widespread popular support, however, and to counter the power advantage of foreign rulers, they had to make promises to their masses and provide the latter with a minimum of political education. In so doing, they of course held out the prospect of *development's benefits for the people.* And, they added, the prerequisite for this happy state was political independence. There was, at that stage, no talk of populist control of indigenous political affairs. Nor was there a fully explicit awareness of the general world forces – market, ideological – which operated to keep a country dependent even after its political autonomy was recognized. The progressive discovery of the persistence of economic dependence, of the structural vulnerability[44] of entire societies in the realms of economics, politics and culture, helps account for the emerging consciousness, on the part of Third World leaders, of the monopoly of control over development processes – at critical points – still detained by their former partners, or by the stronger powers which had supplanted them in choice spheres of influence. And one pervasive arena where such structural vulnerability manifested itself was the arena of world politics and of the Cold War.

This is the main reason why delegates of twenty-seven countries, designating themselves as the Third World,[45] met in Bandung, Indonesia, in April, 1955, to assert a collective identity separate from that of Cold War antagonists, capitalists and communists alike. Accordingly, the Bandung Declaration is, in its own right, another prelude to the emerging consciousness of the under-developed world.[46] The most influential participant of Bandung was China, already firmly held by a Communist government. For almost three decades Chinese Communists had been not only anti-colonialist and anti-imperialist, but advocated a comprehensive total domestic social revolution as well. Such advocacy, along with its immense population and size, explains why China could wield special influence at a gathering of underdeveloped nations. Its own internal revolution introduced explicitly into the development debate the question of internal social reforms elsewhere. Moreover, the fight to oust colonialists and imperialists was viewed as directly related to the struggle for new domestic social structures. Indeed foreign "exploiters" in colonial times had always found native allies to share their privileges. Even after independence foreign powers find it easy to support regimes which do not challenge the basic social and economic structures set in place by the colonizers. Former masters live comfortably with newly independent states, provided these leave unchallenged the former's economic and cultural supremacy. Partly to reverse this trend, countries seek to overcome their state of economic subservience and cultural dependence. One could, in this regard, fruitfully review the collective statements made at successive Third World conferences after Bandung. What emerges is a progressively more explicit affirmation of the right of vulnerable nations to control their own economic destinies. To undertake such a review lies beyond the scope of this paper.[47] The Viña del Mar document cited earlier, however, is a representative example of a more conscious public declaration on the part of non-developed representatives in opposition to their domestication by the developed. Their complaint is not primarily that they are poor, but that they are kept poor by the general structures within which their own development efforts must be deployed.

Similarly, in a document signed by members of seventy-seven nations in preparation for the second UNCTAD Conference held in New Delhi (1968), we read that:

> Although modern technology offers developing countries great possibilities to accelerate their economic development, its benefits are largely by-passing them due to its capital and skill intensive nature, and is drawing away from them such limited skills as are developed.[48]

For the solution to this, as well as to innumerable other problems, they conclude that:

> Traditional approaches, isolated measures and limited concessions are not enough. The gravity of the problem calls for the urgent adoption of a global strategy for development requiring convergent measures on the part of both developed and developing countries.[49]

Third World nations were disappointed at UNCTAD II, however. As one observer has said, "What the developed countries could offer at New Delhi fell so far short of the aspirations of developing countries that the latter were extremely disappointed by the compromises finally agreed upon."[50] The pertinent point here is not that expectations were deceived by performance, but rather that those very expectations are now being articulated collectively in ever more explicit form. Such articulation is a major expression of that emerging consciousness of which I speak. Its expression, moreover, is not confined to the diplomatic language of official documents.

Political leaders in revolutionary societies have given voice to a number of pointed judgments which are widely endorsed by much broader groups in the rest of the Third World, even in non-revolutionary countries. One cultural and ideological illustration is Mao-Tse-Tung's profession of scorn for "Western" democracy. Mao warns his people against the power of mystification which lies hidden in the word as follows:

Those who demand freedom and democracy in the abstract regard democracy as an end and not a means. Democracy sometimes seems to be an end, but it is in fact only a means. Marxism teaches us that democracy is part of the superstructure and belongs to the category of politics. That is to say, in the last analysis, it serves the economic base. The same is true of freedom. Both democracy and freedom are relative, not absolute, and they come into being and develop under specific historical circumstances.[51]

Fidel Castro provides a second example of a fully conscious leader in an underdeveloped country refusing to trade dignity for development.

We have the right to hold our heads high, the right to speak our own opinions and ideas; the right to be an example to any of the small countries in the world, to any of the underdeveloped countries dominated by imperialism or colonialisms in any part of the world. And this also means that we are committed to gain a place in world history.[52]

One is not surprised of course to discover that revolutionary leaders are fully conscious of their nations' vulnerability. What is more significant is the observation that many non-revolutionary leaders are coming to share that consciousness. To illustrate, the authors of Kenya's development plan formally insist on the "need to avoid making development in Kenya dependent on a satellite relationship with any group or groups of countries. Such a relationship is abhorrent and a violation of the political and economic independence so close to the hearts of the people."[53] The sentiment of enlightened leaders in underdeveloped societies likewise finds clear expression in this declaration of a Brazilian bishop as he pleads for a utonomous development:

We do not need paternalistic redemption. We need conditions so that those who are now abandoned may free themselves from their own underdevelopment with their own united force...the poor have no hope in those who still have economic power. And the poor are those who struggle for justice. If those who fight for justice are called subversive, then subversion is their hope.[54]

There is, in short, a larger constituency throughout the Third World for the summons to refuse domestication by those already developed. Domestication is development in the satellitic pattern, within the orbit of some metropole. In addition to its hold on social reformers and many formal leaders in underdeveloped lands, rejection of this view is occurring among a widening fifth column inside the developed world. I speak here of dissident practitioners and insurgent development scholars. For them as for their counterparts in underdeveloped lands, *the key issue of the development debate is control over development processes, not mere sharing in development's benefits.* Within the United Nations, the World Bank, the Agency for International Development, as well as in the universe of development scholarship, one finds individuals working from within to modify their working arrangements with underdeveloped counterparts so as to abolish domestication. Instead of commenting on their existence, however, it is more enlightening to specify the content of the emerging consciousness they share with spokesmen from underdeveloped societies.

Perhaps its most important ingredient is a sense of historical mission. As the English historian E.H. Carr has written: "It is only today that it has become possible for the first time even to imagine a whole world consisting of peoples who have in the fullest sense entered history." Commenting on this text, Heilbroner observes that before the present drive toward development "most of the underdeveloped world had no history" and that "this attempted Great Ascent (is) the first real act of history."[55]

In societies hitherto passive on the historical stage are to become agents of their own destiny, they will have to struggle to overcome their economic, political and cultural vulnerability. Recognition of the need to conduct such a struggle is, accordingly, the second ingredient in the emerging consciousness of the Third World. A third element is the drive toward optimum life sustenance, esteem and freedom; the broad goals of all development efforts.[56] There is greater recognition now than before that it is not worth sacrificing dignity for bread. That is to say, some societies are now prepared to maximize their material achievements at a slower rate than might otherwise be possible at the price of abandoning greater autonomy. Tanzania is undoubtedly the most conspicuous case. The objective is doubtless to achieve development, but not any kind of development and, above all, not development at any cost. What underlies this consciousness, although it is rarely discussed in precise terms, is the aspiration of have-not nations after a new world order. More will be said later about this world order which far transcends present arrangements.

## 2. we are not consumers of civilization

To Senegal's president, Leopold Senghor, is attributed the statement, "We Africans do not wish to be mere consumers of civilization." The phrase, although uttered by a pro-Western non-revolutionary statesman, epitomizes the difference between a domesticated and a liberating form of development effort. Nevertheless, under present rules for bilateral and multilateral transfers (of goods, services, capital, personnel, and information), all important institutions are biased in favor of recipient countries which willingly accept domestication. Accordingly, "donor" countries and agencies are willing to be "generous" in their aid and their investments to partners who will not insist on reciprocity or on the abolition of their own structural vulnerability. But the development effort of the underdeveloped world at large is distorted if these ground rules are perpetuated. Whoever views the recommendations of the Pearson and other major development reports as palliatives can show no enthusiasm for them, notwithstanding their appearance as technically sound and politically moderate. These reports simply have not faced the issue of a broad change strategy implicit in Third World analyses of vulnerability. Nor have they broken new ground in rendering possible the kind of new international division of labor which is needed if authentic world development is to become possible and sketch out the general outlines of an optimum world order.

## 3. change strategies

Any global change strategy aimed at rendering genuine development possible for the entire world must include elements of creative incrementalism as well as certain revolutionary changes. Such a comprehensive strategy is hostile to two viewpoints. The first of these holds that all necessary social changes can be obtained gradually and that there is never any *need* to alter basic structures via those abrupt social mutations known as revolutions. The second view is its opposite: it argues that revolution or some combination of revolutionary programs is *sufficient* to create the worldwide institutions upon which genuine development can be based. It is my belief, on the other hand, that profound changes (some revolutionary, others incremental) are required on several fronts: in the dominant values operative in developed countries; in the social structure of many underdeveloped countries; and in the overarching international arrangements governing worldwide exchanges of technological information, persons, goods and services.

To state the matter differently, development for the whole world at large becomes possible only if three conditions are met:

1. a cultural revolution occurs in the United States and in other developed countries;
2. drastic social revolutions take place in many underdeveloped countries; and
3. there comes into being a new world order qualitatively different from all futures projectible on the basis of present trends.

In a certain number of developed countries, requisite value changes can perhaps be achieved step-by-step without a total subversion of the present order. The same may also be true of the social distribution of power and wealth in some less-developed countries. As for the desired world order, its creation, even over the long term, presupposes a level of international collaboration which far transcends any single program, evolutionary or revolutionary. There are, however, several problems at least which a strategy relying solely on gradualism cannot settle: rigid privilege systems, closed structures of political domination, long-standing structural inequities in differential access to social goods. Revolutions may prove necessary, therefore. On the other hand, to rely on revolution alone as one's integral strategy is to render oneself impotent to solve certain problems whose scale and complexity brings the fate of all mankind into their range. Among these issues are prevention of nuclear war, protection against ecological catastrophe, the assurance of human control over mass technologies, and the discovery of how societies may devise an education for all their members which will not also be a massive brainwash. *Neither incrementalism alone nor revolution alone can be an adequate strategy for making substantial progress on all these fronts.* Therefore, strategists must learn to stock their quivers with incremental, as well as with revolutionary, arrows. Anything less can only be a partial strategy at best, unsuited to dealing with the totality of issues. It is not any form of incrementalism which will suffice, however: one must learn to distinguish between *creative* and *palliative* grandualism.[57]

To accept this distinction is doubtless to have answered a prior question, viz. can gradual progress avoid being mere palliative? Must all cumulative steps toward change necessarily remain at the surface of things and does reliance on gradual processes ineluctably transmute all innovations into mere palliatives? Palliatives are clearly undesirable because they treat the symptoms of evils, never the root causes. Furthermore, palliatives prevent fundamental change by lulling people into accepting minor improvements instead of demanding adequate solutions to problems. As time passes, palliatives worsen the condition they set out to cure, either by raising hopes they cannot satisfy or by tinkering with defective social mechanisms thereby postponing treatment until the disease becomes incurable. Creative incremental measures, on the other hand, are designed to open new possibilities for subsequent radical change, even though at the moment of adoption they appear modest. Indeed, it may well be that of two measures which seem identical at first glance one may, upon further examination, prove to be palliative, the other creative. The difference is that a palliative move reinforces the pathology of the original condition, whereas a creative step, although it may be small if taken by itself, prepares the way toward more comprehensive change. Creative gradual measures harbor that latent dynamism which propels societies beyond immediate problem-solving and renders new futures possible. In this respect, they resemble revolutionary measures which, as Régis Debray puts it, aim at "freeing the present from the past."

Of crucial importance is the ability of the strategist of induced social change to discern which measures bear within them a merely palliative potential, which a creative potential. *Potential* is a term borrowed from physics. The potential energy of a rock that has been poised on the top of a hill for a million years is harmless to anyone. If, on the other hand, its energy can be made kinetic by some random push it can cause a new situation to arise. Similarly, latent social energies remain inoperative unless they are kineticized. In most cases the push is not random or accidental. Nevertheless, randomness or serendipity can at times transform apparently "safe" concessions into explosive revolutionary instrumentalities which go beyond the intentions of their authors. The provision of Western education to elite colonists is one example: although colonizers overtly willed to endow a small number of indigenous personnel with useful skills or congenial cultural aspirations, the education they granted them sowed the seeds of subsequent independence and rebellion. This is not the place to repeat what I have written elsewhere[58] regarding the subjective and objective criteria for deciding when a gradual measure is creative or palliative. Nor can I here undertake to decide which set of conditions create a pre-revolutionary situation and which do not. Even within the arsenal of revolutionaries, moreover, one may prefer violent or non-violent weapons as well as indulge in greater or lesser degrees of violence.[59] For purposes of this essay, it is enough to state that the analysis of underdevelopment outlined above implies a global change strategy which embraces revolutionary measures as well as incremental measures deemed by their authors qualitatively different from mere palliatives. What is also implied is that the major development reports presently under scrutiny do not seriously consider either the possibility of revolution or the distinction between palliative and creative incremental steps.

Inasmuch as many gradual steps can be creative only when allied to a complementary strategy of social mutation (revolution), the analysis contained in most of the reports severely biases their recommendations in the direction of palliative measures. This distortion is a logical consequence of the false imagery of partnership employed by those reports. By ignoring the structural vulnerabilities—economic, political and cultural – which lie at the heart of the experience of underdevelopment, the reports gloss over any possible distinction between palliative and creative incremental change strategies. What is worse, they thereby condemn many of their potentially "creative" recommendations to having but palliative effect. Here lies their fundamental defect.

This weakness most transparently falsifies reality in the disproportion between the pious advocacy of value changes in the underdeveloped countries, coupled with total silence regarding the need for basic value changes within developed countries. Nevertheless, the advice given by representatives of developed to those of underdeveloped countries to optimize resource use and not to waste scarce goods is patently unconvincing when it emanates from men whose own society is profligate in its waste patterns. Likewise, to urge upon Africa, Asia or Latin America the reform of social structures with a view to greater equality and incentives is meaningless advice when the United States itself resists all efforts to restructure its own domestic class arrangements. No less serious is the insistence with which such governments battle to maintain their privileges in international arenas, an attitude analoguous to that of oligarchies in underdeveloped lands. Unless the United States reverses its values, however, and abandons the quest for ever-increasing mass consumption, it will remain trapped by its "need" to scour the world voraciously for raw materials and markets, thereby perpetuating institutional obstacles to the conquest by underdeveloped  nations of growth-producing trade relations with the rest of the world. Still another domain in which a change in values must occur is in the definition of national security. Even for rich and powerful countries national security cannot morally and legitimately be defined simply as maintaining or extending spheres of influence, or of decreeing that development efforts of others will be tolerated only if they do not strenthen ideological claims of some putative enemy. Within this perspective, the social revolution which United States power is now thwarting in Vietnam reflects a tragic ignorance by Americans of the true dynamics of development. Quite obviously, United States leaders will not be ready to judge such social revolutions with a favorable eye until United States public opinion has learned to view United States national security in less megalomaniacal terms. Similarly, the posture adopted by the Soviets in stifling Czechoslovakia's efforts to redistribute internal power as well as to diversify its external financial relations represents an anti-developmental, quite as much as a counter-revolutionary, stance. Hence a profound change in the definition of Socialist leadership as well as in the extent of national claims is needed no less in "developed" USSR than in "developed" USA.

It is likewise apparent that it is senseless for developed leaders to preach restraint in armaments budgets to poorer neighbors unless they reduce their own arms expenditures. More basically still, it is the very conception of the good life prevailing in "have" countries which needs revision. This is so for two reasons: first, because affluence for the entire world is impossible; second, because an unduly materializing image of development reduces all human values to simple accumulation – of capital or of consumer goods. August Hecksher rightly points to the absurdity of surfeit while commenting on the depersonalized abundance which marks life in this country. According to him, the more leisure urban man acquires, the more space he needs simply to store his objects. "He is islanded in an encroaching sea of things. The closets are merely to take the unmanageable excess."[60] The only reasonable target for development efforts in poorer lands is to abolish misery and achieve moderate comfort for all, not to "catch up" with present levels of material abundance in the United States. We are told by the authors of Pakistan's Twenty Year Perspective Plan that "massive improvement will still leave standards far below the level of developed countries. It [achievement of the plan] will, however, eliminate poverty and ensure that at least the basic minimum necessities of life are available to everyone."[61]

Rich countries, on the contrary, need to revamp their own priorities, away from a plethora of trivializing goods in the direction of fewer but more satisfactory objects and services. Implied here quite obviously is a theory of priority needs. Whether an economic system obeys an autarkic subsistence pattern, the law of demand and supply or of central planning, an implicit set of need priorities prevails in the absence of explicit priorities. Under the first system, mass penury confers *de facto* primacy on survival needs. Market arrangements, in turn, favor the production of whatever goods are demanded (although not necessarily needed) by those possessing effective buying power. Finally, rigorous planned economies have concentrated on heavy industry, armament "needs" and collective infrastructure, with heavy stress on bureaucracies. Once the prospect of abolishing basic needs by applying technology becomes realistic, however, in this complex and interrelated world, something more than an implicit theory of needs is required. Explicit policies are required because world resources must not continue to be depleted to satisfy the wants of the few while more urgent and more important needs of the many go unmet. Whatever be the specifics of any priority scheme of needs, it must accept a practical distinction among needs of first necessity, needs which contribute to human enchancement, and luxury needs.

Three policy conclusions flow from recognition of this distinction:

1. The major economic effort of all nations, developed and underdeveloped, should concentrate on providing all men with sufficient first necessity goods. The provision of these essential goods should also serve as the primary target of all regional and international economic policies. Any system or policy which rejects this priority is structurally unethical. It violates two of the normative principles which regulate development efforts: the priority of "being" over "having" in human life, and the principle of optimum universal solidarity.[62] Realistic policy-makers doubtlessly know that abrupt radical change in present practices is not immediately feasible. Nonetheless, acceptance of this priority on principle supplies needed direction for contemplated improvements. Studies already conducted by FAO, UNESCO and other agencies can guide experts in setting quantitative minimum needs in food, housing, health care, educational services, and other goods in this category.

2. A second priority task for worldwide economic effort is to facilitate for all men the access to goods which enhance men's human potentialities -- intellectual, emotional, cultural, expressive, creative, and spiritual. Inasmuch as no universal norms are binding in this domain nor are needs static, it follows that permanent instruments of popular consultation must be created at many levels if social planners are to be simultaneously realistic and non-elitist. The desired outcome of such consultation is a qualitative judgment

regarding enchancement needs directly related to human development, maturation, actualization, and fulfillment. Cultural diversity as well as some measure of personal idiosyncrasy must here be safeguarded. Nevertheless, existing patterns of mass-consumer economies are clearly incompatible with the fulfillment of this second category of needs, which stand highest on a scale of intrinsic importance. Economist Benjamin Higgins is not mistaken when writing that "development is the human ascent, the ascent of all men in their quintessence of humanity, including the economic, biological, psychological, social, cultural, ideological, spiritual, mystical and transcendental dimensions."[63]

3. Only after these two categories of human needs are adequately met for all can one justify major economic effort aimed at producing luxury goods. The contribution of such goods to human well-being is not negligible, it is true; but their disordered use can only perpetuate misery, increase waste, and legitimize alienating structures of consumption, But their use would be disorderly and irrational were they to be given higher priority over other, more urgent and more essential, goods.

Had the Pearson and other reports been faithful to their mandate to constitute a "grand assize" which "takes nothing for granted," they would have seriously explored an operational theory of global human needs. That they failed to do so is not regrettable omission; it is a sign that these reports represent groups with a vested interest in perpetuating the irrational and unjust priorities which govern present world economic activity. Lip-service is given to "partnership" with the Third World, but the need theory which lies implicit in Third World documents and which I have just briefly outlined is studiously ignored. Inevitably, therefore, the reports offer us palliative solutions to monumental problems.

The new world order mentioned above would be characterized by new structures of global productive capacities as a function of these need priorities. Three further conditions would need to be met if successful development is to become a genuine possibility for the totality of mankind: a world development plan, a world technological pool, and new standards of equity allowing different degrees of national sovereignty in nations. Although space is lacking here for a detailed presentation of each, a brief outline is indicated.

Wherever need is pressing and resources are scarce, economic rationality imposes planning as a strict necessity. These conditions prevail in the world taken as a whole. Moreover, local, national and supra-national regional plans cannot be coordinated in the absence of a world plan. Underdeveloped countries' own efforts at rationality are often thwarted by influences operating outside their own boundaries and to which they remain highly vulnerable. Accordingly, their efforts need to be buttressed by world structures aimed at mobilizing human creativity and regulating access to resources in accord with priority needs. One understands, therefore, why Myrdal, Tinbergen, Perroux, Lebret and other development writers have long urged the adoption of a world plan. International development policy, Tinbergen tells us, "should show an improvement in the distribution of world incomes, that is, a more rapid growth of incomes per head in the developing nations than in the developed countries."[64] He adds that planning is concerned with "the whole economy and even with a considerable part of society"; moreover, "the basis of qualitative planning is the theory of welfare economics."[65] I do not believe, however, that the ideal goal of world planning is to create a worldwide welfare state; we must surely go, as Myrdal's book title suggests, *Beyond the Welfare State.* Tinbergen is right, on the other hand, in viewing a world indicative plan as a necessary counterweight to "the junglelike behavior of national governments."[66] The tasks facing world planners will be multiple:

-- to specify the aims of international economic policies.

-- to exert pressure on developed countries to accept greater burdens in removing the stigma of underdevelopment from the world

— to avoid duplication in national planning efforts,

— to provide a coherent supply of market analysis materials to public and private exchange units, and

— to contribute in a problem-solving mode, to the establishment of an international order consonant with the international flow of social influences and technology.

Although he clearly grasps the difficulties of implementation, Professor Tinbergen judges that "the difficulties are not insurmountable." He feels encouraged by the work of the United Nation's Center for Development Planning, Projections and Policies, seeing in its activity a preliminary exercise clearing the way for truly international planning machinery. More recently, Tinbergen has advised the United Nations' Economic and Social Council to study the

> coordination of the Indicative World Plan for Agriculture with the objectives of the Second Development Decade, industrial development strategy, international division of labor, transfer of technology and technical assistance, regional economic

co-operation, priorities with regard to policy measures and arrangements for appraisal of progress during the Second Development Decade.[67]

A world plan would be futile, however, in the absence of new global financing arrangements and a world technological pool. I will say nothing further here on financing; the reader is referred to the larger work mentioned above.[68] But the technological pool scheme merits a word of description here.

What the British call the "migration of minds," Americans designate as the "brain drain." Under either name it signifies the veritable torrent of skilled men from all lands who congregate in deployment of their skills, not where needs but where rewards are greatest. Even more visibly than in the case of investment capital, the circular causation mechanisms postulated by Myrdal are at work here. This is why, if the world's human resources are to be utilized in accord with global need priorities, new mechanisms must be invented for locating trained personnel where they are most urgently needed to perform essential priority tasks. A world technological pool must be created because neither the international market demand system for brainpower nor the closed nationalistic disciplinary policy has proved successful. It must be clearly stated at the outset that the creation of a world technical pool does not, and need not, presuppose the existence of a world government. What I contemplate is a worldwide arrangement, perhaps on a voluntary basis at first, wherein each important technical sector and unit (whether that unit is national, multinational or local) would assume partial responsibilities for conducting research, supplying services and producing goods on a non-profit basis for the international community. This is obviously very different from a world welfare state scheme which would employ every engineer, chemist, pharmaceutical researcher or fertilizer expert on this planet in a single agency. Rather, what is sought is the operation, beyond national boundaries, of the principle now accepted within them: namely, that economic units be induced by fiscal and other incentives to contribute to society's overall welfare. According to French economist Francois Perroux:

> *Capital transfers without compensation seem destined to become a procedure which is not exceptional and, of necessity, a school for solidarity. They will necessarily lead to the exploitation of a layer, which still lies dormant and sterilized nowadays, of altruistic motives which it is perfectly unjustifiable not to use economically.*[69]

However impractical a world technological pool may appear, worldwide economic rationality is impossible without it. More importantly, many underdeveloped nations are condemmed to being second-rate societies in a technological world ruled by a coalition of powerful national interests (public and private) and multinational units (corporations and international technocratic bureaucracies). Precise working modalities of such a pool have yet to be invented, but realistic strategy dictates that innovative efforts build incrementally on extant practice. At the very least, radically new recruiting procedures in the United Nations and other technical assistance agencies might begin to generate progress in the right direction. The professionalization of technical assistance as a trans-national career would no doubt also help. National governments themselves, foundations, universities, research organizations, and industrial units must learn to subsidize and provide other incentives to experts (their own and others not on their payroll) who donate their efforts to the envisaged pool. Trans-national training programs will also be needed, aimed at eliciting from scholars and technicians the commitment to labor for the pool whenever they leave their own country either to further their education elsewhere or to enjoy superior research facilities. Multiple experiments will surely be needed before even the most qualified and creative experts shall have chartered the course. But Perroux is right: it is high time for experts to make room in their theories and policies for the economic resource and mode of exchange heretofore known as the "gift."[70]

I have in these paragraphs pleaded the case for a world plan and a technological pool and, without supplying details, have also argued on behalf of new global financing arrangements. Notwithstanding their importance, none of these matters is discussed by the development reports, with the exception of those prepared for the United Nations. This is why, notwithstanding their real limitations, the United Nations documents are less palliative in their total impact than Pearson, Peterson, Perkins, Hannah, CED, and the others. At least the United Nations documents betray some sensitivity to the worldwide structures of vulnerability which domesticate many development efforts. Yet they too are timid in dealing with international aid, displaying no concern for breaking the monopoly of technical and economic power held by the coalition just evoked and which looms so imminently on the horizon: the alliance of world technocratic elite classes, public and private servants serving national and multi-national masters. Indeed, all that I have recommended above remains merely palliative unless new ground rules governing national sovereignty come into being.

What appears to be, but in truth is not, a double standard for nationalism must become normative. Fragile entities must be allowed to become more nationalistic so as to achieve that emotional integration which is a strong prerequisite for national development. For their part, "developed" nations must partly curtail their sovereignty in order to begin rendering possible the existence of a new world order with its world plan, world financing and world technological pool. Underdeveloped countries have now won general acceptance at least in principle, for differential tariffs, on grounds of equity and to protect their embryonic and fragile industries. In similar fashion, they must pressure world assemblies to admit the two-tiered principle of national sovereignty. Whether a particular developed nation is capitalistic or communistic, ideologically fervent or tepid, the pursuit of a "national interest" defined by itself necessarily consolidates, in our kind of world, the structures of vulnerability which keep the have-nots in a state of dependence. The nationalism of the developed and the allegiances which it nurtures need to be relativized.[71] Concretely speaking, several powers which have traditionally fallen within the domain of sovereign nation-states must be removed from national decision-makers. These include major decisions regarding technical transfers, access to the world's resources, massive investment across boundaries and other moves whose impact on the development possibilities of vulnerable societies cannot be allowed to remain in the hands of those who already control development's macro-dynamisms and harvest a disproportionate share of its benefits. To put it bluntly, they must have their national sovereignty reduced because they too easily harm the Third World, even when they "innocently" pursue putative "national interests."

Underdeveloped nations, on the contrary, often need more nationalism for a time in order to mobilize the energies of their people around the great myth of development. Furthermore, their capacity to cause serious damage to others in their international relations is minuscule. I speak here solely of sectors of policy directly related to development. Quite obviously, also, no meaningful steps toward the world order here described is possible until serious disarmament becomes a reality. We are thus faced with a paradoxical situation. Most development reports, conscious of the difficulty of getting the big powers to disarm, project a world order which is only slightly more efficient than the one now available. They do this in the name of realism. Yet it is totally unrealistic to imagine that genuine development (development marked by autonomy for all societies, cultural and ecological diversity, non-elitist institutions for decisionmaking) can occur unless the structural changes just sketched out take place. One's initial response to such measures is to question their feasibility. Without a doubt, they will never become feasible as long as the sages entrusted with missions of periodic evaluation continue to "think small" and imagine that politics is the art of the possible. In a world of drastically speedy change, the only viable politics is the art of expanding the frontiers of possibility. If one seriously heeds the warning of Barbara Ward and others that our "spaceship earth" is now making a perilous crossing through the unique historic space known as the revolution of rising expectations, it is evident that the stewards of world development have had a failure of nerve, of imagination, and of political will. Although they repeatedly tell us in their reports that development depends above all on decisive will, they themselves refuse to tamper -- even conceptually -- with a present world order completely unsuited to provide anything more than domesticated development to a few "lucky" Third World nations. Their timidity is attributable, not so much to their failure of vision, as it is to the implicit self-knowledge of these leaders themselves. They cannot help perceiving that they too are part of the domesticated development establishment. The Pearson Report offers a tell-tale sign of such recognition when, after warning that development "will be untidy, uneven, and ridden with turmoil" it concludes that "if the developed nations wish to preserve their own position in that world, they must play their full part in creating a world order within which all nations, and all men, can live in freedom, dignity, and decency (p. 11)."

The burden of my argument is precisely the opposite: that a world order in which freedom and dignity are possible for all nations and all men is *not* one in which developed nations will be able "to preserve their own position." Their position is one of disproportionate power and wealth. To improve the lot of those at the bottom of the ladder will necessarily alter the absolute and relative position of those already developed. The greatest tragedy is not that the Pearson statement is representative of the view found throughout the documents. What is more serious is that few less developed societies enjoy any leverage to counter this dominant approach.

# V

## conclusion:
## the development debate

Two questions lie at the heart of the development debate: (1) Can poor societies obtain both development's benefits and control over the social processes which generate these benefits? (2) Is the world now on its way to achieving development? Some form of development is universally assumed to be desirable because underdevelopment is viewed as an intolerable condition. Beyond this, however, there is sharp disagreement. Optimistic observers hold that we have now learned much about development and are on our way, provided we muster up sufficient will and creativity, to succeeding. Others condemn all past efforts and present plans as radically insufficient. They do not deny that vast sums of money and enormous energies have been expended to improve production and social conditions in many lands. Nor do they overlook the fact that industry and new institutions have found root in many "traditional" soils. Nevertheless, they conclude that authentic development has not taken place.

One spokesman for this view is Dudley Seers, Director of the Institute of Development Studies, University of Sussex and former Director-General of the Planning Staff of the United Kingdom Ministry of Overseas Development. Here are his sober words on the subject:

> Since development is far from being achieved at present the need is not, as is generally imagined, to accelerate economic growth – which could even be dangerous – but to change the nature of the development process . . .One cannot really say that there has been development for the world as a whole, when the benefits of technical progress have accrued to minorities which were already relatively rich, whether we are speaking of rich minorities within nations or the minority of nations which are rich. To me, this word is particularly misleading for the period since the war, especially the 'development decade' when the growth of economic inequality and unemployment must have actually accelerated (I am alarmed at the phrase, a 'second development decade.' Another 'development decade' like the 1960's with unemployment rates and inequalities rising by further large steps, would be politically and economically disastrous, whatever the pace of economic growth!)

Certainly in some respects, as I have said, a basis has been laid in many countries for possible development in the future. But there has not been any basic improvement in international institutions.[72]

Similar doubts are voiced by Myrdal in his latest work; he wonders whether "developing countries are really developing."[73] According to him, the optimistic bias of development literature has blinded experts to the need for radical reform within underdeveloped countries. But the trouble goes much deeper, and not even Myrdal himself calls sufficient attention to the need for radical changes in international structures. Nor does he ask whether "developed" countries have truly developed. As these structures now stand, they serve as obstacles to global development. Throughout this essay I have stressed the difference between the benefits of development and autonomous control by societies over development processes. On neither count, adequate benefits or optimum control, have past efforts succeeded. And none of the projections contained in the numerous development reports deals adequately with these two dimensions of the development task.

The major effort must undoubtedly come from less-developed countries themselves; even at best aid can only be a secondary element in an overall development strategy. Nevertheless, it seems utterly callous for spokesmen from the developed world to set an "optimum" target for aid at 1% of the rich countries' gross national product. "In Fy [Fiscal Year] 1970," we are told by Robert McNamara, "the AID programs constitute less than one-fifth of 1 percent of the GNP, and less than 1 percent of the total federal budget. The United States now ranks ninth in the proportion of GNP devoted to aid."[74] Such paltry performance evokes an ironic comment once made by Galbraith:

We are led, as a nation, by our present preoccupations, to adopt numerous of the least elegant postures of wealth. Though we have much, and much of the remainder of the world is poor, we are single-mindedly devoted to getting more. This is for the satisfaction of wants which our well-being has induced or which – and the advertising art is not one which by its nature can be concealed – we have synthesized. And we are, on the whole, rather solemn about the whole process.

We do, each year, provide some aid for others. But first we have a prayerful discussion of whether or not we can afford the sacrifice. . .The nineteenth–century plutocrat who devoted his energies to expanding his already considerable income, who was led by his competitive position in the plutocracy to live on a suitably ostentatious scale; who found, as a result, that his income was never entirely adequate; who came to the aid of the poor only after a careful consideration of their worth, his ability to spare from his needs and the realistic likelihood of revolt and disorder if he abstained; and who believed withal that God inspired his enterprise and generosity and often said so, was not in all respects an attractive figure. Thus with nations.[75]

Moreover, the cost of aid to recipient nations often proves exorbitant. Myrdal tells of a Pakistani government report prepared in 1958 which reckoned the average cost per American expert placed at its disposal to be $40,000. Understandably, "the Pakistanis implied that they could buy such services very much cheaper elsewhere, if they instead were given the dollars for free use."[76]

Therefore, even the "generous" figure of 1% projected by the reports is derisory. Instead, the widening gap between developed and underdeveloped nations needs to be attacked from the top as well as from the bottom of the scale. Development experts are prodigal in their schemes to build up less-developed nations' capacity to grow more quickly. But they are silent regarding the need to slow down developed nations' growth rate at the same time. Both the absolute and relative gaps are widening. In the words of McNamara, the per capita income gap

is already more than $3,000. Present projections indicate it may well widen to $9,000 by the end of the century. In the year 2000, per capita income in the United States is expected to be approximately $10,000 in Brazil, $500; and in India, $200.[77]

There are no valid grounds for assuming that austerity is for the poor only, but not for the rich. Blindness on this issue is doubly paradoxical, for a slowdown in consumption within developed countries, provided it is wisely directed, could greatly reduce waste, pollution, and destructive social competition. More importantly, it might help create general conditions favoring, for millions of over-developed human beings, less alienated lives. The thinking of the stewards of development wisdom is partisan not only at the level of development benefits (the domain of consumption), but at that of structures of autonomy and dependence as well (the realm of effective power). They never apply the advice they give to the underdeveloped to their own societies.

## domesticating the third world

There exists one empirical case -- monumental in size and importance -- of an underdeveloped country which has rejected the "normal" ground-rules of development. This is China. Its effort to achieve progress toward autonomous, mass-participation development gives primacy to cultural factors (creating new values in the "new man") over mere economic efficiency. This occurs in spite of China's formal adherence to an ideology which views culture as a mere derivative expression of material infrastructures. There is here an important lesson for the entire world: namely, that the changes required in the social relations between developed and under-developed nations are as drastic and far-reaching as those instituted within Old China's internal class structure. This is why I plead for a new world order wherein the Third World's chances of achieving authentic development are optimized. I repeat here what I have said above -- that under present arrangements only a few "lucky" underdeveloped countries can achieve development's benefits. For most others, such benefits will remain out of reach. Relative deprivation, at least, will continue to be their lot. More impor-tantly, most low-income societies will prove unable to reap even modest benefits except in a satellitic relationship to developed metropoles injurious to their aspirations after cultural and political identity. To state it in other terms, bread and dignity alike will prove unattainable for many, whereas for a few the refusal to insist on dignity will guarantee a portion of bread. *This, I contend, is the central issue in the development debate: not birth control, foreign aid, or growth rates. The discouraging truth is that development processes now operative impede the genesis of development for all men.*

One dramatic expression of this dilemma is the antagonism of two powerful historical trends. On the one hand, *technology* emerges as the principal instrument of redemption from misery. Concurrently, however, technology's inner dynamics thrusts all societies toward *elitist* patterns of social organization at all levels of decision-making. As a result, within national societies and in the larger arena of relations among societies as well, those who already have much stand to gain the most from future progress. The Pearson Report alludes to the problem in these terms:

> expenditure for research and development in Latin America amounts to only some 0.2 percent of GNP, while in Asia such expenditures fall between 0.1 percent and 0.5 percent of GNP. In Africa, except for some programs sponsored by industrialized countries, public and private outlay for research and development is negligible. Comparable figures for the

Soviet Union and the United States are 4.2 percent and 3.2 percent of GNP respectively, and for most European countries between 1 and 2 percent.

As the ability to analyze scientific, technical, and managerial problems and propose new solutions has grown in industrial countries, low-income countries have become increasingly dependent on a technology conceived and produced outside their borders and without reference to their special needs.[78]

Mr. K. B. Asante of Ghana has given eloquent voice to the sentiments of underdeveloped peoples in the face of technology's triumphs. He writes:

Our world is polarized into the haves and the have-nots. It would be wonderful if Neil Armstrong spoke for all mankind when he said on landing on the moon "one small step for man; one giant step for mankind." Though I was excited and sat with my eyes glued to television until the early hours of the morning, I did not feel he spoke for me. I do not belong to that part of mankind. But I and countless others want to belong to one mankind.[79]

The elitist trend inherent in technology is alarming because a major ingredient of the great development awakening is the desire on the part of vulnerable individuals and powerless groups alike to become *agents* of their own historical destinies. This dream will be frustrated, however, unless the structures of vulnerability which keep them dependent upon technology's leaders are reversed. The development reports have simply not faced this issue.

I commented earlier on the different vantage points of the development reports and of critical leaders in underdeveloped lands. The authors of the reports see underdevelopment essentially as a *problem* to be solved, whereas for vulnerable, underdeveloped people it is a *trauma* to be overcome. Whoever views underdevelopment primarily as a problem, however, will quite logically seek the most efficient solutions. This means he will try to maximize technological progress, even at the risk of placing societies on the road leading to technocratic elitism. Conversely, to portray underdevelopment as a triple shock of cultural, economic and political vulnerability which perpetuates dependence and poverty is by that very fact to predispose oneself to favor solutions which minimize elitism even at the sacrifice of some technological efficiency. Human liberation in all its dimensions is sought even above abundance. The debate launched into the public arena in 1956 by Jacques Ellul in *The Technological Society* now takes on global proportions. The issue is indeed whether technology can assure man's happiness only at the price of his liberty. The enormity of the challenge is evident since the task is to optimize technological application in a mode which enhances all men's quest for optimum life-sustenance, esteem, and freedom. Institutions need to be structured in such ways as to harness technology to the development cause in a manner which expands solidarity, assures the primacy of the human good over material goods, and counters elitism. Otherwise, development can only fail or give birth to new servitudes.

Nothing is gained by underestimating the intrinsic difficulty of the development enterprise. And policy options are distorted if one maintains a diplomatic silence in the face of embarassing truths. In this regard, the Pearson Report fails egregiously. To cite but a single example, in its discussion of Africa it mentions Portuguese Angola and Mozambique and white-governed Rhodesia, South, and South-West Africa. And we are told:

> This latter group is not treated here.
>
> While it is convenient for discussion to treat Africa as a single region, it is important to recognize that the major sub-regions are distinct and have different development and aid experiences. Any division is bound to be arbitrary.[80]

"Different development and aid experiences" indeed! And the statement that "any division is bound to be arbitrary" is beyond challenge. We have here an instance of a critical ommission -- in this case, of the structures of dependence prevailing in that sub-region of Africa -- induced by the special vantage point of the authors of the reports.[81] One indication of the narrowness of viewpoint which prevails in the reports commissioned by United States agencies is the simple fact that the President of the Bank of America, Rudolph A. Peterson, has served as chairman in the preparation of the report which bears his name, and as a member of the Perkins Report and of the CED (Committee for Economic Development) Report.[82] My reason for denouncing discrete silences when they mask unpleasant realities is that development always has some "winners" and some "losers." Histroical development in the past has been won by England, the United States and other nations at somebody's expense: at the expense of the colonies, a poorly-paid internal or immigrant proletariat or weaker trading partners. But what seems to characterize today's global conjuncture is that there are no longer enough willing victims at whose expense development can be won. Not that authentic development need be exploitative of course. This is indeed the major theme of this paper. And, in truth, technology does hold the promise of creating almost unlimited new wealth. But that new wealth will simply enrich those already privileged *If Present Ground Rules Governing International Exchanges Prevail.*

The solution does not lie in redistributing present wealth. Beside being impossible, such a scheme solves nothing fundamental. But it is no less erroneous to imagine that development can come to the world at large merely by a trickle-down process from productivity gains won thanks to new technology. The basic structures of access to resources, to technological innovation and to decision-making regarding their allocation must be radically altered. In addition, a worldwide revolution in the very concept of what development is and what its proper goals are must take place. The objective cannot be mass-consumer abundance for all, but rather the abolition of misery and alienation for all. Alienation wears many masks: it can afflict the affluent no less than the deprived, the master as thoroughly as the victimized servant.

Behind the global drive toward development lies a great historical question: Can human reciprocity become universal? Or is it condemned to operating only on a limited, and limiting, scale? Can development, in other words, become possible for all men, or must it remain the privilege of only a few -- a few individuals, a few interest groups, a few nations? To cite Robert McNamara once again, "if we achieve the 'quantity' goals, and neglect the 'quality' goals of development, we will have failed. It is as simple as that. We will have failed."[83]

Mr. McNamara is a good diagnostician. But the Pearson Report addressed to him, as President of the World Bank, has not risen to the challenge. It has been said that the 1960's were "A development decade without a development policy."[84] The reports have now supplied the experts with a policy. But it is a policy for domesticating the Third World's development efforts. Recommendations which sound good turn out to be palliatives because they ignore structures of dependence and uncritically share the value assumptions of those who have a vested interest in maintaining control over the dynamisms of development now operative.

Domesticated development is no longer acceptable, however, morally, politically, psychologically. Given the emerging state of consciousness in the Third World, I doubt that it is any longer possible.

# APPENDIX A
## major development reports
## and presidential messages

### Peterson Report
**U. S. Foreign Assistance in the 1970's: A New Approach.** Report to the President from the Task Force on International Development. March 1970. 30 cents. Government Printing Office, Washington, D.C. 20402:

### Jackson Report
**A Study of the Capacity of the United Nations Development System.** (Two volumes.) A report to the UNDP Administrator by R.G.A. Jackson. November 1969. Geneva, Switzerland.

### CED Report
**Assisting Development in Low-Income Countries: Priorities for U. S. Government Policy.** September 1969. $1.24 Committee for Economic Development, 477 Madison Avenue, New York, N.Y. 10022.

### Pearson Report
**Partners in Development.** Report of the World Bank Commission on International Development. September 1969. $2.95. Praeger Publishers, 111 Fourth Avenue, New York, New York 10003.

### Rockefeller Report
**The Rockefeller Report on the Americas.** The official report of a U. S. Presidential mission for the Western Hemisphere. August 1969. $1.25. Quadrangle Publishers, 12 East Delaware Place, Chicago, Illinois 60611.

### NPA Report
A New Conception of U.S. Foreign Aid. March 1969. $1.00 (Special Report 64). National Planning Association, 1606 New Hampshire Avenue, N.W. Washington, D.C. 20009.

### CIC - AID Report
**Building Institutions to Serve Agriculture.** A summary report of the Committee on Institutional Cooperation and AID on a rural development research project. September 1968.

**Perkins Report**
**Development Assistance in the New Administration.** A summary report of the President's General Advisory Committee on Foreign Assistance Programs, October 1968. Reprinted by AID, Washington, D.C.

**The American Assembly Papers**
**Overcoming World Hunger,** edited by Clifford M. Hardin. 1969. $1.95 Prentice-Hall, Inc., Englewood Cliffs, New Jersey.

**Hannah Report**
**International Development Assistance,** January 1969. A statement by the task force on international developmental assistance and international education of the National Association of State Universities and Land-Grant Colleges, Washington, D.C.

**IWP**
**Provisional Indicative World Plan for Agricultural Development.** (Three volumes.) Food and Agriculture Organization of the United Nations.

**PDSC Report**
**The World Food Problem.** A report of the President's Science Advisory Committee. May, 1967. Vol. 1, 60c. Vol. 2, $2.75. Vol. 3, $1.25. Government Printing Office, Washington, D.C. 20402.

**Tinbergen Report**
Committee for Development Planning, Chairman, Jan Tinbergen, **Report on the Fourth and Fifth Session** (17-21 March 1969 and 7-16 May 1969) Economic and Social Council, United Nations, Document No. E/4682, New York, 1969.

**Viña del Mar Report**
**The Latin American Consensus of Viña del Mar,** Latin American Special Coordinating Commission (CECLA), Viña del Mar, Chile, May 17, 1969.

**Statements by the President**
**Action for Progress for the Americas.** October 31, 1969, 20c. Government Printing Office, Washington, D.C. 20402.

**World Trade Policies.** November 18, 1969. House Document No. 91-194.

**U. S. Foreign Policy for the 1970's: A New Strategy for Peace.** February 18, 1970. 75c. Government Printing Office, Washington, D.C. 20402

**Presidential Message to Congress on Population.** July 18, 1969. Printed copies available from Population Crisis Committee. 1730 K Street, N.W. Washington, D.C., 20402

**Economic Report of the President.** February 1970. $1.50. Government Printing Office, Washington, D.C. 20402.

## notes to goulet

[1]Sir Robert Jackson, *A Study of the Capacity of the United Nations Development System,* United Nations Document No. DP/5, vol. 2 (Geneva, 1969), p. 63.

[2]*International Development Review,* vol. 10, No. 1 (March 1968), 43-52.

[3]Gunnar Myrdal, Preface to *Asian Drama,* vol. 1 (Pantheon, 1968), p. xii.

[4]The document is dated May 17, 1969.

[5]Lester B. Pearson, Chairman, *Partners in Development, Report of the Commission on International Development,* (Praeger, 1969), p. vii. Henceforth referred to as *Pearson Report.*

[6]*Pearson Report,* p. ix.

[7]For a balanced treatment of how the anti-Socialist bias misrepresents the performance of the world's most populous' country, cf. John W. Gurley, "Maoist Economic Development, the New Man in the New China," *The Center Magazine,* vol. 3, no. 3 (May, 1970), 25-33.

[8]This question is discussed briefly in Denis Goulet, "The United States: a Case of Anti-Development," *Motive,* vol. 30, no. 4 (January, 1970), 6-13.

[9]On this, cf. the title essay by Douglas V. Steere in *Development For What?* ed. by John H. Hallowell (Duke University Press, 1964), 213-235.

[10]On this, cf. Denis A. Goulet, "Voluntary Austerity: the Necessary Art," *The Christian Century,* 83, No. 23 (June 8, 1966), 748-752.

[11]*Pearson Report,*p.125.

[12]"A Fresh Look at Goals and Next Steps for International Development," A Quaker International Affairs Leadership Seminar, April 24-26, 1970, Capahosic, Virginia.

[13]For extensive discussion of these questions, cf. Denis Goulet, *The Cruel Choice,* (Atheneum, forthcoming).

[14]*Pearson Report,* p.69.

[15]*The Latin American Consensus of Viña del Mar,* p.2.

[16]*Pearson Report,* p.53.

[17]Cf. Jacques Freyssinet, *Le Concept de Sous-Développement,* (Mouton, 1966), *passim.*

[18]*Pearson Report,* p.5.

[19]*Ibid.*

[20]Michael Hudson, review of the *Pearson Report* in *Commonweal* (March 27, 1970).

[21]*Pearson Report*, p.124.

[22]David Hapgood, ed. *The Role of Popular Participation in Development*, M.I.T. Report No. 17, (1969), p. 10.

[23]On this, cf. forthcoming book mentioned in n. 13.

[24]*Pearson Report*, p. 218.

[25]*Ibid.* p.219.

[26]*Ibid.* page 211.

[27]Gunnar Myrdal, *Economic Theory and Underdeveloped Regions* (London: Duckworth, 1957), p.7.

[28]Ivan Illich, "Outwitting the 'Developed' Countries," *The New York Review of Books* (November 6, 1969). Italics added.

[29]For statistics on the relative contribution of the U.S. and other donors, cf. Organization for economic cooperation and development, *Development Assistance, 1969 Review* (Paris, 1969), and Vassil Vassilev, *Policy in the Soviet Bloc on Aid to Developing Countries* (Paris: OECD, 1969).

[30]*Pearson Report*, p. 215. Italics in original.

[31]Committee for Economic Development, *Assisting Development in Low Income Countries: Priorities for U. S. Government Policy* (September 1969), p. 61. Italics in original text.

[32]One major advocate of the beneficence of the multinational corporation is Neil H. Jacoby, former economic advisor to President Eisenhower. For his recent views, cf. "The Multinational Corporation," *The Center Magazine*, vol. 3, no. 3 (May 1970), 37-55.

[33]At the Quaker Conference already mentioned above, Jan Tinbergen argued convincingly that public enterprise in Holland was frequently more efficient and productive than parallel private ventures. All depends, therefore, on the quality of each kind. At stake ultimately are the larger social implications of allowing private, profit-seeking units such disproportionate power.

[34]*The Latin American Consensus of Viña del Mar*, p. 9, paragraph 33.

[35]Denis Goulet, "A Missing Revolution," *America*, 114 (April 2, 1966), 438-39.

[36]Seymour Melman, "Industrial Efficiency Under Managerial vs. Cooperative Decision-Making: A Comparative Study of Manufacturing Enterprises in Israel," undated manuscript, *mimeo.*

[37]Karl Mannheim, *Freedom, Power and Democratic Planning,* (Routledge and Kegan Paul Ltd., 1951), p. 191.

[38] Neil H. Jacoby, *op. cit.,* p. 47.

[39]Ibid., p. 47.

[40]Columbia University, New York, and Institute of International Politics and Economy, Belgrade, *Joint Business Ventures of Yugoslav Enterprises and Foreign Firms,* edited by Wolfgang Friedmann and Leo Mates (Belgrade, 1968), p. 37; cf. also p. 39.

[41]On this, cf. Paulo Freire, *The Pedagogy of the Oppressed,* Herder and Herder, 1970, Also his *Educación como Practica de la Libertad* (Caracas: Ediciones Nuevo Orden, 1967).

[42]See, v.g., Pablo Gonzalez-Casanova, "Internal Colonialism and National Development," in *Latin American Radicalism,* edited by I.L. Horowitz, J. de Castro and J. Gerassi (Vintage Books, 1969), 118-139.

[43]For a detailed exposition of this view, cf. Jacques Freyssinet, *Le Concept de Sous-Développement, op. cit.*

[44]The Structures of vulnerability are discussed at length in Denis Goulet, *The Cruel Choice,* (Atheneum, forthcoming).

[45]On the origins of the term *Third World,* cf. George Balandier, *Le Tiers Monde* (Presses Universitaires de France, 1956), "Introduction."

[46]On Bandung, cf. George McTurnan Kahim, *The Asian-African Conference,* (Cornell University Press, 1956).

[47]The reader is referred to Henri Bazin, "De Bandoung a New Delhi, l'Evolution des Rapports entre les pays du Tiers Monde," *Développement et Civilisations,* no. 33 (March 1968), 13-26.

[48]"Charter of Algiers," UN Document MM/77/I/20 dated 30 October 1967, p. 3.

[49]*Ibid.,* p. 5.

[50]Guy F. Erb, "The Second Session of UNCTAD," *Journal of World Trade Law,* Vol. 2, No. 3 (May/June, 1968), p. 352.

[51]Anne Fremantle, Ed., *Mao-Tse-Tung, an Anthology of His Writings,* (Mentor Books, 1962), p. 268.

[52]Fidel Castro, *Apply Theory to the Particular Conditions of Each Country,* (Republic of Cuba, Ministry of Foreign Relations), text (in English) of speech delivered on January 2, 1965, pp. 18-19.

[53]Republic of Kenya, *African Socialism and its Application to Planning in Kenya* (1965), p. 8.

[54]Dom Antonio Batista Fragoso, "The Gospel and Social Justice," speech delivered in Belo Horizonte (Brazil) on January 22, 1968, *mimeo.* The theme of subversion as an institution-building agency of development is expounded in Orlando Fals Borda, *Subversion and Social Change in Columbia* (Columbia University Press, 1969).

[55]Robert L. Heilbroner, *The Great Ascent,* (Harper Torchbooks, 1963), p.9. The citation is from E. H. Carr, *What is History?* (Alfred A. Knopf, 1962), p. 199

[56]For a treatment of development goals, cf. Denis A. Goulet, "Development for What?," *Comparative Political Studies,* Vol. 1, No. 2 (July, 1968), 295-312, and "On the Goals of Development," *Cross Currents,* Vol. 18, No. 4 (Fall, 1968), 387-405.

[57]This distinction is explained at greater length in Denis Goulet, "Is Gradualism Dead?," *Ethics and Foreign Policy Series,* (Council on Religion and International Affairs, 1970).

[58]Goulet, "Is Gradualism Dead?," *op. cit.*

[59]For one example of graduated violence, cf. Albert O. Hirschman, "Revolution by Stealth: The Case for Sequential Reforms," in *Economic Development, Evolution or Revolution?,* ed. by Laura Randall, (D. C. Heath, 1964), 76-105.

[60]August Heckscher, *The Public Happiness* (Atheneum, 1962), p. 61.

[61]Cited in *Government of Pakistan, The Third Five Year Plan (1965-1971)* (May, 1965), p. 18.

[62]These principles are discussed at length in the work cited above, Denis Goulet, *The Cruel Choice,* chapter 11.

[63]Benjamin Higgins, *Economic Development, Principles, Problems and Policies,* rev. ed. (Norton, 1968), p. 369.

[64]Jan Tinbergen, *Development Planning* (McGraw-Hill, 1967), p. 196. For further details the reader is referred to Tinbergen, "Wanted: a World Development Plan" in *International Organization,* edited by Richard N. Gardner and Max F. Millikan, vol. 22, no. 1 (Winter 1969), 417-431.

[65]Tinbergen, *Development Planning,* p.194.

66*Ibid.* p. 211.

67Committee for Development Planning, Chairman, J. Tinbergen, *Report on the Fourth and Fifth Sessions,* ECOSOC/UN, UN Publication No. E/4682, (New York, 1969), p. 33.

68Cf. n. 44.

69François Perroux, *L'économie du XX Siècle* (Presses Universitaires de France, 1964), p. 373.

70On this, cf. in particular, Francois Perroux, *Economie et Societé, Contrainte, Echange, Don* (Presses Universitaires de France, 1963).

71A similar conclusion is reached from a different starting point and in a different context by psychologist Erich Fromm. See his *The Heart of Man* (Harper & Row, 1964), chapter 4.

72Dudley Seers, "The Meaning of Development," *International Development Review,* vol. 11, no. 4, (December, 1969), pp.3, 6.

73Gunnar Myrdal, *The Challenge of World Poverty* (Pantheon, 1970), p. 404. For additional comments on this point, see ch. 8.

74Robert McNamara, "The True Dimension of the Task," *International Development Review* (1970/1), p. 4.

75John K. Galbraith, *The Affluent Society* (London: Hamish Hamilton, 1958), p. 140.

76Myrdal, *op. cit.,* p. 350. For further evidence of the high cost of aid to "recipients" see pp. 352-355.

77McNamara, *op. cit.,* p. 6.

78*Pearson Report,* p. 66.

79Cited in *Jackson Report,* vol. 1, p. 55.

80*Pearson Report,* p. 261.

81Of the reports under review the UN documents (Jackson and Tinbergen) are the least objectionable on this count. The Viña del Mar statement obviously differs from the others in that its authors purport to speak for their Latin America constituencies.

82The source of this information is *Foreign Assistance, Opinions on its Future,* a joint publication of Reports and Technical Inquiries Staff, Program Support Group, Foreign Economic Development Service, and the U.S. Department of Agriculture. The document is dated March 1970 but is not otherwise identified.

# the political economy of foreign aid

# by
# Michael Hudson

## introduction

The lay public has been ahead of the economics profession for some time now in sensing the inefficacy of foreign aid. For self-evidently the backward countries have failed to develop. Nor have their governments reexamined their increasingly outmoded doctrines of economic growth. Instead, in the face of tightening constraints imposed by their obsolete resources and social institutions, they continue to permit their economic policy to be steered in accord with the laissez faire, neo-classical doctrines preached by Anglo-American diplomats.

Some of the aid-borrowing countries' official representatives to UNCTAD and other U.N. organizations, such as Raul Prebisch of Argentina, have decried the *results* of these neo-classical policies without perceiving that the problem lies in the conditions of production much more than those of distribution. Thus, their proposals call merely for discretionary income-redistribution within the existing conditions of world production, instead of transformation of the economic environment that has aggravated the divergence in wealth-creating powers between rich and poor nations. Their request for terms-of-trade compensation and other forms of income-transfer is merely a call for charitable palliatives rather than for some more fundamental institutional breakthrough. This is largely the symptom of their own conservatism. For to close the widening international gap in production abilities would entail a radical reorganization of their own domestic institutions as well as those of the international economy. It would shift much of the onus for their failure to develop onto their own political-economic obsolescence, thereby entailing political suicide for less radical governments and their economic spokesmen.

Understandably the developed nations, particularly the United States and Britain, are scarcely any more eager to dismantle the postwar international economy that has contributed so greatly to their own development. Thus, there are few official spokesman in either the backward or the developed countries who find their governments' interests to lie in fundamentally altering the existing international economic system. It is less painful for all to negotiate the continued financing of poverty rather than the struggle out of it.

The purpose of this essay is to demonstrate that today's foreign aid programs are more seriously ill-conceived than even the suspicious public and disgruntled congress have grasped. The reasons for their failure to help aid-borrowers to develop lie first in the motives that have governed foreign aid programs since World War II, and secondly in the spurious growth theories called upon to cloak these motives in the guise of altruism. Neo-classical income theory, for instance, has called for an infusion of technological capital (i.e. foreign investment) and Malthusian doctrine for a reduction in population resources, as if such policies could in themselves supplant the need for structural modernization of the backward societies. The situation has been aggravated by the fact that most international economists are plagued by a perverse optimism as to some allegedly natural tendency for all social and economic phenomena to approach "equilibrium" (and ultimately, absolute equality). This curiously optimistic preconception seems to have blinded them from perceiving the steady divergence in productive powers between rich and poor nations, and the consequently self-defeating nature of trying to foster economic development of the latter within the context of an open world economy or without a social revolution to modernize their economic institutions. Unfortunately, economic and political self-interest among the aid-lending nations, particularly the United States, renders their aid-diplomats especially prone to such doctrinal misconceptions.

Part I of this essay discusses the increasingly narrow and para-military self-interest underlying postwar U.S. aid strategy: the movement away from multilateralism to bilateral aid in the immediate postwar years, the tightening of strategic control over these aid programs in the 1960's, and the Peterson Report's plan to revamp the aid program in a multilateral context so as to enlist the resources of the nation's Cold War allies. Public Law 480 is analyzed as a representative aid program that has been achieved at *no* net economic cost to the United States, while having indebted aid-recipient countries to the extent of some $22 billion, thereby tying them to the purse strings of the U.S. State Department and Treasury for nearly twenty years to come.

The U.S. balance-of-payments deficit that has accelerated over the past decade has led the country's strategists to enlist the resources of other nations in support of institutions designed to maintain the world's military and economic status quo and to discourage national planning for social and political independence. Today, the International Bank for Reconstruction and Development (World Bank) and its allied organizations are emerging as the major mechanism for implementing U.S. world designs. Part II of this essay therefore examines the Americanization of the World Bank. The shift in Bank policy under the personal leadership of Mr. McNamara is outlined specifically as it concerns the use of Bank operations to help finance the U.S. payments deficit rather than that of the aid-borrowing countries, and to help finance technological obsolescence in these countries rather than social evolution. The Pearson Report's plan to merge the Bank's operating philosophy into the Pax Americana strategy for the 1970's is also analyzed.

Finally, Part III examines the political and social motivations underlying the State Department's and Bank's (non)growth theory. The anti-developmental aspects of their preferred neo-classical and Malthusian doctrines are seen to reflect the aid-lenders' preference for technological palliatives and population control as alternatives to social and economic modernization in the aid-borrowing countries. For U.S. diplomats suspect that a successful modernization program would presuppose that these countries adopt a protectionist stance, emulating the United States and its industrial allies by forming an economic bloc to promote their own development rather than that of the aid-lending nations.

Before such a political break can take place, a political-economic theory must be developed to supplant neo-classical and post-Keynesian doctrines. This theory will take as its starting point the analysis of why economic evolution in the postwar economy has been just the opposite from that portrayed by neo-classical theory, and why the historical tendency among nations has been for their productive powers to diverge rather than to converge.

We may observe here at the outset that through the mechanism of an open international economy postwar foreign trade, aid and investment have worked to reinforce the international status quo and its inequities. Free trade and open investment policies have tended to aggravate backwardness in the poorer countries. The neo-classical doctrine called upon to endorse this open economy has thus had fundamentally negative political and economic implications for these countries. Asserting itself to be non-political economics, it has turned out to be highly political, self-defeating economics so far as the backward countries are concerned. Its crudely materialistic view of economic stagnation as merely technological in nature has interpreted "slow growth" as resulting simply from too few "capital inputs" with too low productivity. All that seems needed to accelerate the aid-borrower countries' well-being is more capital imports, improved seed varieties, fewer consumers, and tighter austerity to reduce current personal consumption and increase capital formation. The mounting trade deficit is itself recorded in their national income accounts as "capital formation," on the reasoning that it is financed by a "capital inflow" signified by a financial indebtedness to foreign investors and governments. (The political indebtedness it also establishes is dismissed as being political, and therefore exogenous.)

Structural aspects of international aid and investment play virtually no role in neo-classical analysis. Aid discussions are usually couched in broad generalities dealing with the macro-economic aggregates of post-Keynesian GNP analysis rather than with the more subtle categories of classical political economy. For instance, post-Keynesian analysis has dubbed the rate of increase in per capita national income to be the normative criterion of economic growth, irrespective of the inequities in distributing this income, the failure of societies to accumulate capital so as to maintain or accelerate this growth, or their decay of economic self-sufficiency, balance-of-payments equilibrium and monetary stability. No distinctions are drawn between productive and unproductive labor, consumption or investment. In these areas economic literature has lost much of the richness it possessed in the last century. Economists seem to have narrowed rather than broadened their understanding of political-economic evolution.

This limited scope of contemporary economic theorizing did not appear fatal when applied to developed nations following World War II. Because Europe's political and institutional environment was not so rigid as to present an immovable barrier against economic growth, the infusion from the United States of capital equipment and monetary resources was able to play a major role in its postwar reconstruction. It was all too easy to overlook the fact that this tangible capital was applied to a society already rich in the sunk costs of human-capital resources and social-economic infra-

For this reason the backward countries' experience with aid has not been as fortunate as that of Europe. And yet despite its failure to bring them nearer to the day of self-financing capital accumulation they have still not broken intellectually or politically from the aid-lending bloc. They have still not perceived the misconceptions in the theories of development used to rationalize the misdirected aid they have borrowed. Nor have they yet asserted their economic self-sufficiency and political independence from the U.S. economic orbit to be their primary national goal. Quite the contrary, they have permitted twenty-five years of aid-bargaining to indebt them increasingly to the aid-lending bloc. The fact that their debt is increasingly "official" in nature has rendered them subject to all the political and economic strings which have historically characterized such relationships. Ultimately, they have been led to follow a path of economic and social non-evolution that has been dictated righteously by the aid-lending bloc. Rather than adopting policies specifically tailored to their own historical needs they have permitted their national resources to serve the political, economic, and increasingly military world views of the United States and its discouragingly passive allies.

# the role of aid
# in america's postwar strategy

Any loan to a foreign country is nominally recorded as "aid" if it is made within the context of some government program or is approved by some governmental agency. This poses the seemingly absurd situation that if a commercial bank or other private lender finances U.S. exports to Europe or Latin America the loan is recorded as private investment, but if the U.S. government provides the financing or a credit-guarantee through the Export-Import Bank (Eximbank) or th Agency for International Development (AID), or even simply lends its offices as an intermediary in the transaction, the investment is recorded as foreign aid, although it generally entails a much more hardly bargained quid pro quo. Loans and grants associated with the war in Southeast Asia are also treated as foreign aid, with more than half of all U.S. aid in 1968 representing military support assistance. Nor are such practices unique to the United States: Germany France and most other developed nations treat virtually all commercial loans and export-financing to backward countries as aid in their statistical reports so long as these loans can be fit into the context of some government program.

One is therefore tempted to question just what the term *aid* has come to mean. Etymologically speaking, to *aid* means to *add to*, that is, to help. Retrospectively and prospectively, however, what has been helped by U.S. aid programs is the U.S. balance of payments, U.S. industry and commerce, and U.S. long-term strategic goals. The flow of scarce foreign-exchange resources has been from the aid-borrowing countries to the United States. This "aid" has been imposed upon them in the form of a contractual debt service which represents an immense mortgage upon their future balance-of-payments receipts, as well as an immense opportunity-cost of not having acted earlier to guide their economies towards self-sustaining growth.

The "security assistance" that makes up more than half of U.S. aid has not, on balance, fostered these countries' economic and social evolution, but has imposed upon them an expensive and socially destructive military overhead. Export promotion by the developed nations at higher-than-world prices can hardly be considered aid.[1] Food aid which the agriculturally backward countries have received through P.L. 480 has often worked to stave off urgent agrarian reforms. Had these countries chosen not to accept these aid-loans it is not at all unlikely that their economic growth and self-sufficiency would have been greater than that which has in fact materialized: their postwar evolution would have been more inward-looking, and would necessarily have called forth a much more rapid social-economic evolution than has taken place. As events have turned out, technological aid has helped to displace rural peasants and throw them into mushrooming urban slums. The food deficit economies have become increasingly unbalanced and unstable, and in many cases increasingly militarist in nature, particularly for the "forward defense" countries bordering the Soviet Union and China. The strategy of U.S. foreign aid has thus been designed by its diplomats in keeping with its own world policies rather than with a view towards the needs or capabilities of the aid-borrowing countries.

U.S. aid policy during the postwar period reveals a steady tightening of political, military and economic control over all inter-government lending, tying it increasingly to U.S. Cold War strategy. This strategy has been to divide and conquer opponents and allies alike. In the immediate postwar years, for instance, success of the World Bank, the IMF, GATT and other international organizations required Britain's membership and the adherence of her otherwise protectionist sterling area. In a series of bilateral negotiations U.S. diplomats first gained British compliance in a world free trade strategy, and then moved in a united Anglo-American bloc to bargain with the rest of Europe. Then, having acquired European compliance through Marshall Plan aid and NATO military resources, the United States became the spokesman for the industrial nations in a broad wedge against the backward countries, opening up their economies and orienting them to the commercial, raw-materials and strategic military needs of the developed center.

This strategy successfully minimized the development of any organized opposition to U.S. policies. Nation was set against nation and region against region. Today, individual countries may with draw from this incipient "world village" only at the cost of becoming exiles in the world economic community: Cuba, Indonesia under Sukarno, Egypt to an extent after it announced its Aswan Dam project, and the short-lived revolutionary regimes in Brazil and Ghana. (Peru, to be sure, may have inaugurated a new and more enlightened era in U.S. attitudes towards the backward countries. Should it succeed in redirecting its economy without being quarantined economically and politically, it will owe a great debt to Cuba and Vietnam for having paved the way for a reevaluation of U.S. foreign policy.)

## the myth of aid

Viewed in its broad outlines, U.S. foreign aid has been designed to offer a quid pro quo to serve two sets of interest: its own and that of its aid clients. It has provided short-term resources in exchange for long-term strategic, military and economic gains. An open international economy has been brought into being within a para-military alliance that in the eyes of U.S. strategists has exceeded the value of goods and services their government has loaned (and to a much lesser extent given) to other national governments.

Military aid ("security assistance") now accounts for over half (52%) of U.S. foreign assistance. Recipients of this military aid are divided into two categories: the forward-defense countries bordering the Communist bloc, and the less strategically placed countries where threat of Soviet military presence is not so great. Of paramount importance in the forward-defense countries is preservation of the status quo, whatever its implications for their longer-term economic growth. Any disturbance of this status quo, it is hypothesized, might work to Soviet advantage simply by introducing a new risk element into the balance of power.[2] U.S. aid to this military ring is therefore designed above all to minimize the "risk of the unknown" by supporting existing governments, both directly through military arms and personnel transfers, and indirectly through economic aid to mitigate any forces of discontent that might perhaps impel these nations out of the U.S. strategic orbit. This explains U.S. support of the Greek dictatorship, of India, and of the Southeast Asian countries, where economic motives or development potential alone are clearly unable to justify the massive infusion of U.S. resources.[3] In the less strategically located countries this political stasis is less imperative, particularly since Cuba's revolution in 1959 enlightened U.S. aid authorities as to the folly of over-rigidity in international and domestic political-economic relations. More economic criteria may be pursued in determining aid to these more happily situated countries.

Taken on balance, all U.S. foreign assistance is ultimately military or para-military in nature, even its ostensibly economic aid: it is designed primarily to enable foreign countries to support a military superstructure capable of saving the United States the cost of having to provide military service with its own armed forces. In the words of the Korry Report of March 1970, "The magnitude of the U.S. aid effort was largely justified on national-interest grounds, with the annual level determined less by abstract development goals than by the level of additional resources thought necessary to support a military establishment adequate to assure national independence under the U.S. nuclear umbrella."[4] Domestic policing operations to contain revolutionary situations which would threaten the status quo are also promoted. It is hoped, of course, that the aid-client will be able to continue purchasing U.S. exports on commercial terms in accordance with established growth trends, where such trade is possible after sustaining the balance-of-payments costs of its military budget. This commercial benefit now seems secondary to overall strategic aims, however.

Foreign military strength is thus encouraged to the extent that it dovetails into U.S. military objectives and remains dependent upon U.S. control–the NATO pattern of the 1950's. Discouraged, however, are tendencies towards developing an independent military force capable of initiating acts that might not serve U.S. policy ends. The threat of withholding further military and related aid is a major lever in this policy. This is a persuasive bargaining tool in the hands of U.S. military planners, as the existing weapons systems of most non-communist nations are tied to complementary U.S. inputs.

Export promotion ("development assistance") makes up 42% of U.S. aid (the remaining 6% being welfare and emergency relief). Here again U.S. aid-strategists divide client countries into two categories, developed and underdeveloped. The developed nations may at some point put forth national strategies of their own to rival U.S. commercial objectives. This has recently been demonstrated, for instance, by the Common Market in its agricultural policy and its proposed associate membership status for selected African countries (which would, among other things, tend to channel Africa's mineral wealth towards Europe). For the backward countries, by way of contrast, the strategy is not to seek new spheres of influence, but to decide by which industrial sphere to be captured—or else to build a protected regional economy of their own. They may move into the U.S. policy sphere (that of an open international economy revolving around the axis of U.S. commercial supremacy), they may align themselves with some other developed nation or group of nations (as in the prewar sterling and franc areas, or with the Common Market today), or they may develop their own self-contained protectionist regions. Thus, the African ex-colonies are now being obliged to choose between applying for associate membership in the European Common Market, thereby disqualifying themselves from the recently-proposed U.S. special tariff concessions to the backward countries or pursuing an open-door policy towards international trade that would qualify them for special low U.S. tariffs but not for the Common Market's trade preference system.

Economic growth abroad is encouraged, just as is military preparedness, to the extend that it dovetails into U.S. commercial and military objectives—but only to that extent. From the vantage point of U.S. self-interest, optimum foreign growth is often difficult to establish as it tends to be ambiguous in its implications for U.S. commerce. For instance, rising income abroad is viewed as favorable to the United States to the extent that it generates an increasing demand for U.S. commercial exports, but unfavorable to the extent that it is generated or accompanied by a displacement of other U.S. exports. From the U.S. point of view, economic growth abroad would ideally express itself to the greatest possible extent as an increased demand for U.S. commercial exports or in various less direct contributions to the country's balance of payments. Japan's trade surplus with third countries, for instance, benefits the dollar area's balance of payments in the same way that the Arab countries' oil surpluses prior to World War II swelled the resources of England's sterling area, as the net proceeds of its trade are kept in assets denominated in dollars rather than in gold or in non-dollar currencies. Thus, Japan's net trade surplus is partially reflected in a capital inflow to the United States, absorbing liquid dollars from third countries which might otherwise use them as claims on the U.S. gold stock. (As part of the treaty between the United States and Japan which ended World War II, that nation is not permitted to hold gold, and is thus virtually forced into the dollar area.)

In any event it is desirable to U.S. planners that foreign countries' growth be trade-oriented; This helps explain their doctrine that backward countries should foster their growth by transferring resources from this domestic economy to the export sector, pursuing free trade import policies rather than fostering domestic self-sufficiency. These recommendations are made not only through U.S. aid missions directly, but also indirectly via the World Bank and other international lending organizations influenced by U.S. political-economic doctrines. Where export-oriented growth does take place, U.S. negotiators obviously find it preferable that these sales be made by foreign affiliates of U.S. companies, so that the U.S. balance of payments may benefit from the remitted earnings on these sales or the buildup of U.S. capital assets abroad via reinvested earnings. Economic growth of the import-displacing type, by way of contrast—that is, growth in the direction of commercial self-sufficiency—is not in U.S. self-interest, all the less so when foreign-owned firms displace imports from the United States.Whether or not greater dependence on U.S. trade and capital is the conscious motive of development planners, or whether, as is more likely, it is merely the incidental result of promoting "high productivity" (i.e., capital-intensive) industries in the extractive and manufacturing sectors, the effect is a bias of economic growth towards dependency on the international economy rather than on the home market.

Accelerated growth abroad, even where it works on balance to, increase the overall net demand for U.S. goods and services, may be, deemed antagonistic to specific narrow U.S. interests. For instance, the Common Market's agricultural program has generated a demand for U.S. farm equipment, fertilizer imputs and feed grains, but has at the same time displaced other classes of U.S. exports, particularly the softer grains (and now, possibly, soybean oil exports as well). U.S. trade negotiators have responded by somewhat irrationally demanding the best of both worlds: they want Europe to continue increasing its demand for U.S. hard grains and other farm inputs, but they simultaneously request that U.S. soft wheat be guaranteed a fixed proportion of the continent's grain market. For this narrow self-interest there can of course be no altruistic theoretical defense.

To the developed and backward countries alike U.S. negotiators have offered short-term plums sufficiently enticing to exact long-term political-economic adherence to its preferred policies. The most important of these policies is that foreign nations abandon their national long-term economic, military and political self-determination. Towards this end its postwar aid program has been used to discourage growth in all cases where it has threatened to carry foreign countries away from their dependence upon U.S. sources of economic and military supplies--no matter what might be the ultimate long-term benefit to U.S. commerce taken as a whole. (Japan's economic and military resurgence, once again, is fostered to the degree that it contributes to the commercial strength of the dollar area, and its army to the policing of Asia as indicated in President Nixon's 1970 State of the World Message.) At any rate, national self-interest being inherently what its name implies, that is, selfish, it was inevitable that U.S. foreign assistance would come to be used as a lever to thwart economic growth abroad wherever this growth was accompanied by a desire--or even the potential--to attain the same commercial self-sufficiency that has been the aim of U.S. trade policy since the Civil War.

As the United States emerged from World War II, its strategists had already worked out in their minds the Cold War divisions which they expected to characterize postwar society, and which they proceeded, inevitably, to bring into being. They obviously did not desire to continue providing Lend Lease or other forms of aid to the country's nominal ally, Russia, or to its satellites. Nor were they interested in any form of multilateral aid that did not serve bilateral U.S. aims. On May 8, 1945, Lend Lease was terminated, not only to Russia but to England as well.

This curtailed U.S. ability to use aid-bargaining to influence Soviet policy. It also forced Britain to seek a reconstruction loan from the United States--mainly to rebuild its economy at home, to say nothing of its overseas dominions with whom its economic relations were never again to approach prewar levels. In exchange for the $4 billion loan (which was spread over 1946-48), U.S. diplomats obtained Britain's agreement to open its hitherto closed sterling bloc, its oil monopoly in the Middle East, and its spheres of influence in general. The loan conditions contributed to the end of Britain's empire.[5]

In 1946 Secretary of State Clayton withdrew U.S. support from the United Nations Relief and Reconstruction Administration (UNRRA), although contractual U.S. contributions to it and its successor agencies continue at a high level through 1948. From the vantage point of U.S. Cold War strategy the problem of the UNRRA was precisely its multilateralism: it was obliged to distribute aid according to economic need, which meant to Eastern Europe and other areas within the Soviet sphere of influence. (The four largest recipients of UNRRA aid were China, Poland, Italy and Yugoslavia.) Here was certainly a quid without quo so far as U.S. policy aims were concerned.

After 1948 virtually all U.S. aid was bilateral, save for the country's investments in the World Bank and IMF--which worked indirectly to stimulate world demand for U.S. exports and to open up the international economy in accordance with U.S. designs.[6] Apart from the British loan, the major U.S. lending agency was the Eximbank, which provided U.S. companies with about $0.5 billion annually to loan to foreign purchasers of U.S. exports.[7] Until 1954, when P.L. 480 was passed, the remaining U.S. official foreign "nonmilitary" lending comprised mainly program loans under the Mutual Security and related acts. For the period 1948-1960 taken as a whole, mutual security grants amounted to nearly $1 billion annually (accounting for about 80% of total U.S. grants, the rest being mainly P.L. 480 aid). Until about 1952 over

### the political economy of foreign aid

95% of U.S. aid was extended to Europe to help reconstruct its economy, thereby strengthening it as an anti-communist ally by helping to dampen any left-wing pressures that might otherwise have emerged from a situation of general economic discontent, and enabling it to attain the status of a growing market for U.S. exports.

### public law 480:
### its costs to the united states
### and to the aid-borrowing countries

By 1953 European reconstruction was well underway, and attention was turned to the backward countries, which had become the new battleground for social and political-economic discontent. In 1953 the Mutual Security Act was passed, and the following year the Republican administration revamped the country's foreign assistance program. The major innovation was P.L. 480, formally known as the Agricultural Trade Development Assistance Act (its name indicating that what was to be developed was U.S. agricultural exports, not the farm sectors of the client countries). Its subtitle described it as "An act to increase the consumption of United States agricultural commodities in foreign countries, to improve the foreign relations of the United States, and for other purposes."[8] It was designed largely to help dispose of the massive farm surpluses accumulating in the silos and warehouses of the Commodity Credit Corporation (CCC) in a manner less crass than simply burning them or dumping them in the ocean, as had hitherto been the general practice.

The act enabled the U.S. government to aid in the overseas marketing of U.S. farm surpluses by acting as its own foreign exchange broker: the new agency would "purchase" surplus commodities from the CCC and sell them to foreign governments in exchange for their own local currencies (rather than for dollars or other hard currencies). It would then resell these currencies for dollars to other U.S. government agencies and--when the currencies on hand exceeded the governments operating needs--to private U.S. investors and travellers as well.

P.L. 480 rapidly became a major channel for U.S. foreign aid. Today, the foreign currencies received in exchange for its food sales are being expended at the rate of about $300 million annually, being used by eight different U.S. government agencies for some twenty-one different purposes.[9] "Public Law 480-generated foreign currencies," the 1965 annual report observes, "continued to be used to pay embassy operating costs and other overseas expenses of the Government, conserving dollars and strengthening the U.S. balance of payments position. In the last ten years, over $2.7 billion in such foreign currencies have been disbursed in place of dollar payments that would, in almost all cases, otherwise have been made."[10] U.S. government agencies are thus saved from having to throw dollars onto world foreign exchange markets to purchase the client countries' currencies (which could set up potential claims on the U.S. gold stock). The economic effect is thus the same as that of a hard-dollar sale.

A further balance-of-payments contribution of the program is its stimulus to bona fide commercial farm exports from the United States. "Expansion of dollar sales," the 1970 report notes, "owes much to aggressive worldwide development efforts initiated under P.L. 480."[11] This is because, as a precondition for granting P.L. 480 aid, the U.S. Department of Agriculture "develops a program which provides for suitable quantities, *establishes levels of required commercial imports from the United States and friendly countries* (usual marketing requirements), and included self-help measures suitable to the needs of the requesting country."[12] This requirement that foreign purchases of U.S. farm commodities on commercial terms reach prescribed levels is based on the principle of "historical market share": the larger the foreign food market grows, the more it must import from the United States.[13] Hence, the aid-borrower's deficit on food account *must* widen over the years as a *precondition* for obtaining food-aid: it must increase its aggregate farm imports from the United States in accordance with its domestic market growth while its farm exports must not increase (on the ground that they might potentially displace U.S. commercial exports). Meanwhile, it must pay increasing debt service to the United States for the past P.L. 480 food aid it has received.

This hardly seems to be a viable self-help policy: neither the farm sector nor the balance-of-payments position of the aid-borrower is helped. The aid client is contractually obliged *not* to implement policies of domestic agricultural self-sufficiency, but to enter into agreements similar to that which the United States signed with Britain in 1968 assuring it a "guaranteed market-share" and which it attempted to sign with the Common Market, but which that entity recognized would effectively preclude the Common Agricultural Policy and its associated farm-income and price support program. "Self help" must therefore be narrowly constrained within existing income and distribution patterns, that is, in the context of a continued deterioration of the backward countries' farm-trade account. Indeed, the major self-help policies suggested tend to be those which contribute to the U.S. trade and investment position, particularly the fostering of technology-intensive farm investment: the planting of new hybrid varieties of wheat and other crops, for instance, entails the importation of new seeds and farm machinery from the United States.[14]

During 1955-69 P.L. 480 accounted for some 23% of total U.S. farm exports. "Mutual security" food sales extended through the State Department (AID) accounted for 4%, and raw materials barter programs (Defense Department) for another 2% (Table 1). Thus all government export programs taken together accounted for some 29% of total U.S. farm exports.[15] (This ratio was even higher during the 1950's averaging some 36%.

**the myth of aid**

TABLE 1 Value of U.S. farm products shipped under Public Law 480 compared
with total exports of U.S. farm products, July 1, 1954 through December 31, 1969  1/

(In millions of dollars)

| Calendar year | | Public Law 480 | | | |
| --- | --- | --- | --- | --- | --- |
| | Sales for foreign currency | Long-term dollar and convertible foreign currency credit sales | Government-to-government donations for diaster relief and economic development | Donations through voluntary relief agencies | |
| 1954 July-December......... | -- | -- | 28 | 20 | |
| 1955 ................................ | 263 | -- | 56 | 186 | |
| 1956 ................................ | 638 | -- | 65 | 187 | |
| 1957 ................................ | 760 | -- | 39 | 175 | |
| 1958 ................................ | 752 | -- | 43 | 159 | |
| 1959 ................................ | 732 | -- | 32 | 111 | |
| 1960 ................................ | 1,014 | -- | 49 | 124 | |
| 1961 ................................ | 878 | 1 | 93 | 151 | |
| 1962 ................................ | 1,006 | 42 | 81 | 178 | |
| 1963 ................................ | 1,161 | 52 | 99 | 160 | |
| 1964 ................................ | 1,233 | 97 | 62 | 186 | |
| 1965 ................................ | 899 | 152 | 73 | 180 | |
| 1966 ................................ | 815 | 239 | 79 | 132 | |
| 1967 ................................ | 736 | 193 | 108 | 179 | |
| 1968 ................................ | 540 | 384 | 101 | 150 | |
| 1969 ................................ | 335 | 427 | 103 | 153 | |
| July 1, 1954 through December 31, 1969... | 11,762 | 1,587 | 1,111 | 2,431 | |

1. Export market value.

2. Annual exports have been adjusted for 1963 and subsequent
years by deducting exports under barter contracts which improve
the balance of payments and rely primarily on authority other
than Public Law 480. These exports are included in the column
headed "Commercial Sales."

3. Sales for foreign currency, economic aid, and expenditures
under development loans.

| Barter 2/ | Total Public Law 480 | Mutual security (AID) 3/ | Total agricultural exports | | | |
|---|---|---|---|---|---|---|
| | | | Total Government programs | Commercial sales 4/ | Total agricultural exports | Public Law 480 as percent of total |
| 22 | 70 | 211 | 281 | 1,304 | 1,585 | 4 |
| 262 | 767 | 351 | 1,118 | 2,081 | 3,199 | 24 |
| 372 | 1,262 | 449 | 1,711 | 2,459 | 4,170 | 30 |
| 244 | 1,218 | 318 | 1,536 | 2,970 | 4,506 | 27 |
| 65 | 1,019 | 214 | 1,233 | 2,622 | 3,855 | 26 |
| 175 | 1,050 | 158 | 1,208 | 2,747 | 3,955 | 27 |
| 117 | 1,304 | 157 | 1,461 | 3,371 | 4,832 | 27 |
| 181 | 1,304 | 579 | 1,483 | 3,541 | 5,024 | 26 |
| 137 | 1,444 | 35 | 1,479 | 3,555 | 5,034 | 29 |
| 37 | 1,509 | 11 | 1,520 | 4,064 | 5,584 | 27 |
| 43 | 1,621 | 23 | 1,644 | 4,704 | 6,348 | 26 |
| 19 | 1,323 | 26 | 1,349 | 4,880 | 6,229 | 21 |
| 41 | 1,306 | 47 | 1,353 | 5,528 | 6,881 | 19 |
| 13 | 1,229 | 33 | 1,262 | 5,118 | 6,380 | 19 |
| 3 | 1,178 | 11 | 1,189 | 5,039 | 6,228 | 19 |
| -- | 1,018 | 5/ NA | 1,018 | 4,918 | 5,936 | 17 |
| 1,731 | 18,622 | 2,223 | 20,845 | 58,901 | 79,746 | 23 |

4. Commercial sales for dollars include, in addition to unassisted commercial transactions, shipments of some commodities with governmental assistance in the form of short-and medium-term credit, export payments, sales of Government-owned commodities at less than domestic market prices, and, for 1963 and subsequent years, exports under barter contracts which benefit the balance of payment and rely primarily on authority other than Public Law 480.

5. Not available.

**the myth of aid**

The P.L. 480 crop-disposal program has been achieved at virtually no economic cost to the United States, as detailed in Chart 1. One of the reasons is that the country's farm surpluses would have been purchased by the CCC as part of the country's farm-price support program, irrespective of whether or not they could be marketed abroad. In fact, "operations under Public Law 480 have assisted in reducing costs to the American taxpayer of storing and servicing food surpluses."[16] According to the Peterson Report, the economic shadow cost of making these export sales is only 50% of their nominal aid-transfer price, as "More than half the budgetary cost would be required in any event to support farm incomes in the United States."[17] Thus, the effective cost to the United States of its $16.2 billion in P.L. 480 crop disposal program through 1969 was cut by some $8.1 billion.

Furthermore, the government disbursed some $3.0 billion of its foreign currencies obtained through the program to its various agencies, sold $0.5 billion to private enterprise, and expended some $1.3 billion for "common defense" through the Pentagon (mainly in Korea and Vietnam). $1.7 billion was used by the Defense Department for strategic raw-materials barter. Long-term dollar and other convertible currency sales made up another $1.6 billion, so that the total balance-of-payments credits amounted to $8.1 billion, just matching the domestic $8.1 billion in what the CCC would have had to expend to store or otherwise dispose of these crops.

These computations do not include the agency's re-lending of the program's remaining foreign currency holdings to foreign governments for their own use (and eventual repayment). Since the inception of the program such loans have amounted to some $5.6 billion for "economic development" purposes. The United States thus in effect gets paid more than once for its P.L. 480 exports: once in foreign currency for its crop exports, and again when its re-lent currencies are paid back. In this manner its pool of foreign currencies is kept intact.

Largely because this self-replenishing nature of P.L. 480's foreign currency holdings and assured the U.S. government of abundant foreign-currency resources for years to come, a policy change was enacted in 1966 calling for the State Department to shift completely to hard-currency sales by 1971.[18] Thus, by 1969, "Among Title I sales agreements made with 22 countries only six provided for any local currency financing (Ghana, India, Korea, Pakistan, Tunisia and Vietnam), and only one exclusively (Vietnam)."[19]

## Chart 1

### COST-BENEFIT ANALYSIS OF P.L. 480 AID: 1955-69

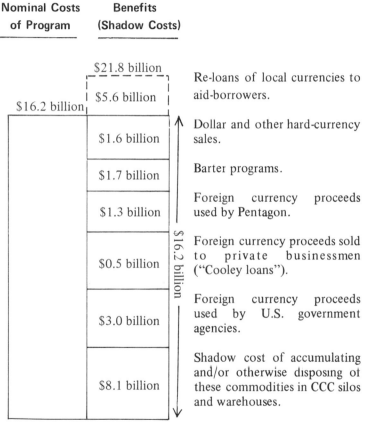

| Nominal Costs of Program | Benefits (Shadow Costs) | |
|---|---|---|
| | $21.8 billion | |
| | $5.6 billion | Re-loans of local currencies to aid-borrowers. |
| $16.2 billion | | |
| | $1.6 billion | Dollar and other hard-currency sales. |
| | $1.7 billion | Barter programs. |
| | $1.3 billion | Foreign currency proceeds used by Pentagon. |
| | $0.5 billion | Foreign currency proceeds sold to private businessmen ("Cooley loans"). |
| | $3.0 billion | Foreign currency proceeds used by U.S. government agencies. |
| | $8.1 billion | Shadow cost of accumulating and/or otherwise disposing of these commodities in CCC silos and warehouses. |

Source: 1970 report, Tables 1, 13 and 16.

Note: Private donations made through the P.L. 480 program (for instance, through CARE, the Red Cross, Catholic Relief Services, etc.) are excluded from these statistics. These private donations amounted to some $2.4 billion during the life of the program.

Among the domestic currency expenditures under the P.L. 480 program are "Market development projects (which) include sponsoring trade mission tours of the United States by foreign buyers, participation in trade fairs overseas, and publicity and advertising campaigns. Promotional activities reach 70 countries. Some 40 private U.S. agricultural trade and producer groups were working on continuing project agreements with the Department of Agriculture's Foreign Agricultural Service. . . ."[20] Section 104(b)(1) of P.L. 480 "provides that not less than 5% of these currencies may be used to maintain, expand, or develop foreign markets for U.S. agricultural commodities,"[21] with some $116 million having been spent for such purposes since the program's inception. Four tobacco export associations are cooperators in this P.L. 480-sponsored market development program, and among the commodities financed through P.L. 480 sales have been $24.5 million in tobacco (half of it going to Vietnam), although the positive role of tobacco in economic development has yet to be demonstrated. In past years the *Congressional Record* has contained annual humorous statements (wittingly and unwittingly) by Southern representatives asserting how tobacco exports indeed help stimulate foreign economic development by relaxing foreign labor or by stimulating it to work harder, etc. Such statements may not be in keeping with the U.S. Health, Education and Welfare Department's stance on the tobacco question. In 1969 the Mink Breeders Association joined the P.L. 480 overseas marketing program, presumably enlisting the services of U.S. minks in fostering economic progress abroad.

Self-interest of a political-economic nature was also written into the act through the Hickenlooper Amendment, which until 1968 (when Peru successfully challenged it) called for food and other forms of aid to be hung as a kind of Sword of Damocles over the heads of client countries. Any foreign country that nationalized U.S. investments without satisfactory (to the U.S. investor) compensation would have its aid withheld. In principle, the riskiness of U.S. foreign investments in the backward countries was thereby reduced, although U.S. profits did not fall correspondingly in recognition of this reduced risk.[22]

## overall contribution
## of the u.s. foreign aid program
## to the country's balance of payments

In 1961 the incoming Kennedy administration revamped the aid program, centralizing all activities in the State Department under the newly-created Agency for International Development (AID). The most important economic aspect of the new aid program was its enlistment of aid activities to help reduce the mounting pressures on the U.S. balance of payments. Unless the payments deficit was overcome, U.S. strategists recognized, a transfer of economic and diplomatic power to continental Europe would take place in proportion to the flow of gold. To "aid" lower-income clients without further strengthening Europe as an economic rival, all aid was tied to the purchase of U.S. goods and services, except for specifically military or paramilitary assistance to Asia where security aims outweighed those of economics. A Gold Budget was established as an accounting control device to maximize the aid program's balance-of-payments contribution.

New export-credits under all U.S. aid programs now called for foreign-currency counterpart funds. In addition, all aid-commodities had to be shipped in U.S.-flag ships, for which freight rates were substantially in excess of going world tramp rates. Thus in 1961, if official Department of Commerce figures are accurate, some 39% of total U.S.-flag ships' receipts from foreigners on ocean freight derived from the transport of U.S. aid-commodities.[23]

In order to make certain that no displacement of commercial exports took place, foreign aid was subjected to what was termed an "additionality" provision: "Additionality measures were an attempt to prevent AID financing of goods that might otherwise have been exported through regular commercial transactions. The principal device used was limiting the selection of U.S. products permissible for AID financing to those in which the U.S. share of the local commercial market was small, so that AID-financed imports of these products would very likely be additional to normal commercial purchases from the United States."[24] By 1968 U.S. aid was contributing massively to the balance of payments, accounting for a $904 million *surplus* entry–the amount by which the $1.5 billion received by U.S. aid agencies in the form of interest in principal repayments on past U.S. aid exceeded the balance-of-payments cost of new aid, as 95% of this new aid was tied directly to purchases of U.S. goods and services (Chart 2 and Table 2).[25]

*Chart 2*

# BALANCE OF PAYMENTS EFFECT OF U.S. GOVERNMENT SECTOR

(amounts in millions of dollars)

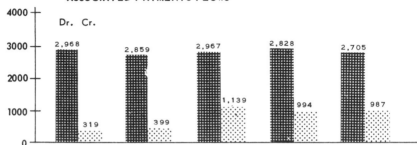

MILITARY TRANSACTIONS AND THEIR
ASSOCIATED PAYMENTS FLOWS

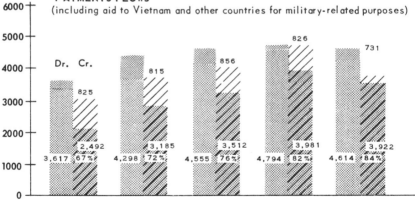

NONMILITARY GRANTS AND LOANS AND THEIR ASSOCIATED
PAYMENTS FLOWS
(including aid to Vietnam and other countries for military-related purposes)

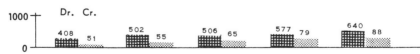

OTHER U.S. GOVERNMENT SERVICES AND TRANSFER PAYMENTS

NET LOANS ACTIVATED UNDER SWAP AGREEMENTS ( OUTFLOW )
(equals "increase in official holdings of convertible currencies")

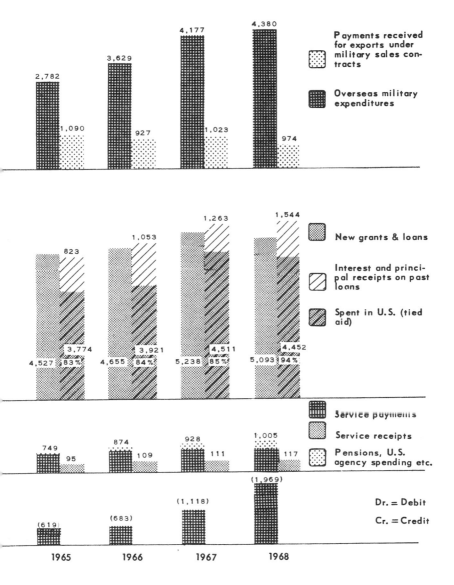

2,782  3,629  4,177  4,380

Payments received for exports under military sales contracts

Overseas military expenditures

1,090  927  1,023  974

1,263  1,544

823  1,053

New grants & loans

Interest and principal receipts on past loans

Spent in U.S. (tied aid)

3,774  3,921  4,511  4,452

4,527  83%  4,655  84%  5,238  85%  5,093  94%

Service payments

Service receipts

Pensions, U.S. agency spending etc.

749  874  928  1,005
95  109  111  117

(1,969)

(1,118)

(683)

(619)

Dr. = Debit

Cr. = Credit

1965    1966    1967    1968

95

TABLE 2 "Foreign Aid" in the
(millions

NONMILITARY GRANTS AND LOANS, and their associated payments-flows

1. New grants and other capital outflows: net funds spent abroad
   (O.B.E. Table 5, line 34)

   A. Total new grants and capital outflows[1]

      1. Nonmilitary grants
      2. Loans and other long-term assets
      3. Net foreign currencies and other assets (increase)
      4. *Less* credits to finance military sales contracts
         (O.B.E. Table 5, line A.29 = B.4)
         Memo: Foreign currencies used by U.S. Government other
                  than for grants or credits (O.B.E. Table 5, line A.23)

   B. Spent in the United States[2]
      1. On merchandise exports (O.B.E. Table 5, line A 27)
      2. On services (O.B.E. Table 5, line A.28)
         a. Transport
         b. Private services
         c. Interest on prior U.S. Government credits
            (O.B.E. Table 5, line A.6)
         d. U.S. Government services
         e. All other services, n.i.e.
      3. U.S. Government credits to repay prior U.S. private credits (mainly bank
         credits) (O.B.E. Table 5, line A.31)
      4. U.S. Government credits to repay prior U.S. Government credits
      5. Increase in U.S. Government liabilities associated with specific grants and
         capital outflows (O.B.E. Table 5, line A.32)

2. Income received on U.S. Government loans and other assets, net

   A. Total
   B. Financed by U.S. Government credit
      (O.B.E. Table 5, line A.6)

3. Net receipt of principal repayment on past credit (scheduled only)

   A. Total
   B. Financed by new U.S. Government credit (line 6.p) (O.B.E. Table 5, line A.30)

Source: O.B.E. Table 5, and unpublished O.B.E. estimates.

[1] Equals O.B.E. Table 5, line A.1 less line A.29, plus A.23
[2] Equals O.B.E. Table 5, line A.26 less line A.29.

## U.S. Balance of Payments
## of dollars)

| Reference to O.B.E. Table 1 | 1960 | 1961 | 1962 | 1963 | 1964 | 1965 | 1966 | 1967 | 1968 |
|---|---|---|---|---|---|---|---|---|---|
| | (300) | (329) | (186) | 13 | 40 | 70 | 319 | 537 | 903 |
| | (1,125) | (1,144) | (1,042) | (813) | (691) | (753) | (734) | (726) | (641) |
| 29*, 42*, 43* | (3,617) | (4,298) | 4,555 | (4,794) | (4,614) | (4,527) | (4,655) | (5,238) | (5,093) |
| 29 | (1,664) | (1,853) | (1,919) | (1,917) | (1,888) | (1,808) | (1,910) | (1,802) | (1,706) |
| 42 | (1,213) | (1,939) | (1,129) | (2,201) | (2,375) | (2,454) | (2,501) | (3,634) | (3,713) |
| 43 | (528) | (261) | (245) | (447) | (19) | (16) | (265) | 209 | 72 |
| 42* | 26 | 33 | 13 | 36 | 16 | 90 | 291 | 390 | 554 |
| 43* | 238 | 278 | 275 | 265 | 349 | 340 | 270 | 401 | 300 |
| | 2,492 | 3,185 | 3,512 | 3,981 | 3,922 | 3,774 | 3,921 | 4,511 | 4,452 |
| 3* | 2,046 | 2,396 | 2,503 | 2,882 | 3,032 | 2,952 | 3,152 | 3,523 | 3,331 |
| | 368 | 497 | 670 | 785 | 690 | 748 | 798 | 767 | 855 |
| 6* | 162 | 218 | 230 | 252 | 244 | 209 | 192 | 185 | 200 |
| 9* | 75 | 75 | 75 | 75 | 75 | 75 | 75 | 75 | 75 |
| 13* | 69 | 74 | 114 | 147 | 168 | 183 | 181 | 171 | 196 |
| 10* | 102 | 109 | 130 | 157 | 177 | 190 | 217 | 224 | 235 |
| 60* | 40 | 21 | 121 | 154 | 26 | 91 | 133 | 112 | 149 |
| 38* | – | 111 | 93 | 34 | – | 5 | 14 | 104 | 116 |
| 44* | 37 | 71 | 100 | 186 | 151 | 154 | 162 | 201 | 148 |
| 56* | 41 | 80 | 147 | 94 | 49 | (86) | (205) | (84) | 2 |
| | 279 | 307 | 357 | 351 | 288 | 326 | 412 | 467 | 569 |
| 13 | 348 | 381 | 471 | 498 | 456 | 509 | 593 | 638 | 765 |
| | (69) | (74) | (114) | (147) | (168) | (183) | (181) | (171) | (196) |
| 44* | 546 | 508 | 499 | 475 | 443 | 497 | 641 | 796 | 975 |
| 44 | 583 | 579 | 599 | 661 | 594 | 651 | 803 | 997 | 1,123 |
| | (37) | (71) | (100) | (186) | (151) | (154) | (162) | (201) | (148) |

Thus do the aid-borrowing countries finance their own submission, and thus has the U.S. foreign aid program been one of the major sources of *strength* in the nation's balance of payments, remunerative investment rather than a net economic cost.

P.L. 480 aid was transferred out of the Department of Agriculture into the State Department so as to integrate export promotion more conveniently with diplomatic aims. This centralization of all foreign assistance within AID reinforced its political leverage in securing leases on military bases, signatures on international diplomatic agreements, and the general military and political loyalty of foreign governments.[25] Meanwhile, the Peace Corps replaced the more belligerent gloves of pre-war diplomacy, and paid political dividend at home by attracting the support of many groups that would have opposed increased military involvement abroad. Aid strategy was shifted to emphasize economic development as a social rather than a merely military alternative to communism. The threat to the status quo among America's aid-clients, it was recognized, was becoming more internal than external in nature, more political than overtly military.

This somewhat broadened scope of Cold War aid strategy was defended with disarming simplicity on the grounds that it would contain revolutionary aspirations abroad, by ameliorating the most immediate effects of poverty. In this vein the U.S. Secretary of Defense Robert McNamara asserted, in his congressional testimony on the Foreign Assistance Act of 1964, that:

> In my considered judgment, this (military assistance) program, and the foreign aid program generally, has now become the most critical element of our overall national security effort....If we are to meet the avowed Communist threat across the entire spectrum of conflict, then we must also be ready to take whatever measures are necessary to counter their efforts to promote guerrilla wars and insurrections. And much of this task can be accomplished only by the assistance, both military and economic, we give our less prosperous allies....As President Johnson recently stated, the foreign aid program is the best weapon we have to insure that our own men in uniform need not go into combat.

After the May 1965 buildup in Vietnam, however, the days of bilateral aid were numbered, thereby curtailing U.S. ability to directly manage its foreign assistance program. In 1966 President Johnson asked Edward Korry to draft a new aid strategy to "multilateralize" the foreign assistance program. Korry's report was followed by that of Sir Robert Jackson for the United Nations in 1968, and by another prepared by a committee headed by James A. Perkins, president of Cornell University and a director of the Chase Manhattan Bank. By this time anti-war sentiment had come to threaten the entire aid program, inducing the Perkins Committee to conclude that "Fundamentally the committee believes that development cooperation provides the U.S. with an alternative to military involvement for playing a continuing role in the less developed world. Doves or Hawks on our military commitment in Vietnam can equally support assistance for development."

### the peterson report and its strategy
### for maximizing u.s. self-interest
### in the 1970's

When the new Republican administration took office in 1969 a revamping of the U.S. aid program once again seemed inevitable. The failure of past aid to help its recipients develop had generated a growing reaction against bilateral aid. Furthermore, opposition was mushrooming in Congress to the President's increasing military commitment of the nation's resources. If the overall aims of U.S. aid strategy were to be pursued into the 1970's, they would have to submerge themselves in the anonymity of formally multilateral programs. Not only might this mobilize foreign official resources to supplement those of the United States in pursuing its world designs, but it would also be freer from political opposition at home to U.S. involvement abroad.

In the fall of 1969 President Nixon appointed a fifteen man commission, headed by Bank of America president Rudolph, Peterson, to draft the outlines of this new aid strategy. Mr. Peterson had made headlines in the arena of international diplomacy on April 6, 1967, by suggesting that if Europe threatened to cash in its unwanted dollars for U.S. gold (thereby constraining U.S. economic and political options), the United States should respond by refusing to sell gold, thereby cutting the dollar loose from gold altogether and ultimately letting it float against the European and other currencies.[28] Thus, Europe could not move to dump its dollar holdings and constrain U.S. deficit policies without cutting its own throat. This proposal (which was bolstered later in the week by a similar suggestion made by John Deaver of the Chase Manhattan Bank) signified that the era of bargaining and promises concerning U.S. balance-of-payments policy was over. The country had given notice that it was henceforth going to act without any economic constraints. The beggar-my-neighbor era of the 1930's was upon the world once again.

Also joining the Peterson Commission was David Rockefeller, who held a similar views, and Robert V. Roosa, who while with the Federal Reserve Bank of New York had developed the network of central bank swap agreements in the 1960's that had helped finance the United States payments deficit with Europe's funds. The fourth economist on the commission was the free trade theorist Gottfried Haberler of Harvard. Nine businessmen and two professors rounded out the committee.

The Peterson Report was released in April 1970. Its keynote was that the era of blatant bilateralism was over and that a new low-profile policy was now needed to wrap United States strategic ends in a multilateral wrapping. "A predominantly bilateral United States program," it asserted, "is no longer politically tenable in our relations with many developing countries, nor is it advisable in view of what other countries are doing in international development."[29] As an alternative it drafted a militant strategy on four fronts:

1. to transfer the disposition of foreign aid from the Legislative to the Executive arm of the government, so as to bypass mounting congressional opposition to the President's use of aid-strategy as a vehicle for expanded paramilitary involvement abroad;
2. to adopt a "low-profile" military posture by inducing foreign governments to employ local personnel to supplant United States troops in existing and future military involvements (i.e., the "vietnamization" of foreign military activity);
3. to use bilateral and multilateral aid as an economic lever against the European Common Market; and
4. to implement a more enlightened strategy against social revolution abroad and its associated threat of nationalism and regional blocism.

*1. The Struggle between Congress and the Executive.* "Presidential interests in international development are not adequately served by existing decisionmaking machinery," the report asserts.[30] It recommends that direct control over foreign aid be removed from Congress and turned over to the Secretary of State, so that the President can direct the foreign assistance program more closely. The impetus for this recommendation, of course, was the growing congressional opposition to the illicit seizure of power by the Executive arm of government in involving the nation in foreign wars: "Since 1965, the proposals for foreign aid put forward by the President have met with more and more difficulty. In 1968. . .as always, there was considerable talk about rat-holes, dictatorships, corruption, balance of payments, the threats of communism, the brotherhood of man, India, and the responsibilities of global leadership. . . . And pent-up dismay over the Vietnam situation found an outlet in attacking foreign aid."[31]

To preempt congressional budget cuts in the United States, foreign aid program, and at the same time to reduce the program's net burden to the reported federal budget, the Peterson Commission suggests founding a new aid-lending agency, the International Development Bank (IDB), which could issue its own public bonds not subject to congressional funding or approval. Thus, whenever Congress might tighten the leash or vote against and given strategic use of foreign assistance, the IDB might go to private lenders, both in the United States and abroad.[32]

*2. The Shift towards a Low-Profile Military Involvement Abroad.* The commission believes that the United States can now phase out its military grant program, as the country's allies are now so wedded to U.S. weapons systems that they have little choice but to depend on United States hardware. Easy-credit policies employed by the Defense Department in past years to finance military sales abroad have succeeded in establishing United States arms as the basis for most non-communist armament systems. Replacement demand alone locks these nations into dependency on United States military supplies. The path has thus been paved from aid to trade: "In the past, these countries needed the close involvement of U.S. military advisers to ensure the effective integration of United States arms and equipment into their forces. By now, however, military officials in most of these countries have achieved adequate levels of professional competence and facility with modern (i.e., U.S.) arms."[33] Military grants in the future "should be determined on a cost-benefit basis. The risks involved for the United States and the need for United States forces that would arise if funds were not provided should be specified." In other words military aid should henceforth be granted only in the event that if it were not extended, the Pentagon would have to itself supply United States soldiers bearing United States arms. (The Defense Department demands payment for its arms grants and sales, but not for the lives of its soldiers. When arms are sold to foreign governments, payment with interest is due the United States. Hoever, when the United States sends its soldiers along with their arms, no such payment is requested, and no such debt established. Lives are thus free, weapons [unless borne by U.S. soldiers] are not.)

The new strategy requires foreign countries to take over their own military burden. The U.S. will provide, at a price, the military systems, and foreign countries will provide the military manpower. Security assistance in the 1970's, the report concludes, aims "to improve the military defenses of our allies and move them toward greater military self-reliance, to serve as a substitute for the deployment of U.S. forces abroad, to pay for U.S. base rights, and to deal with crisis situations."[34]

*3. The Political-Economic Struggle against the Common Market.* A major impulse for the Peterson Report's emphasis on multilateralism is its desire to shift the burden of financing U.S. world strategy onto Europe's shoulders. Thus, whereas the Kennedy administration's tied-aid policies were designed simply to prevent the expenditure-benefits of U.S. aid from spilling over to Europe, the Nixon strategy is more aggressively designed to involve Europe's treasuries in the U.S. foreign loan program, while submerging specifically U.S. policies in a new, less visibly self-interested context.

The move towards multilateralism is endorsed *only* on the condition that the European countries agree to untie their aid financing: "If the United States were to act alone in changing many of these practices, it would yield trade and financial advantages to the other industrial countries. . . ."[35] U.S. strategists have apparently computed that the United States would be the major beneficiary of generally untied aid policies, given the established buying practices and channels which its past aid has helped to bring about. Just as aid has financed U.S. weapons systems abroad in the military sector, it has also contributed heavily towards realigning Latin America's import policies towards U.S. suppliers. Thus, "The balance-of-payments cost to the United States of this proposal is estimated to be relatively small." When account is taken of the net expenditures of foreign currencies (or foreign-owned dollars) on U.S. goods and services, and the interest premiums to be paid on this aid-financing, the effect is in fact positive.

The Peterson Report is not unmindful that this interest and principal burden lies heavily upon the shoulders of the backward countries. "The debt burden," it observes, "was foreseen, but not faced, a decade ago. It stems from a combination of causes: excessive export credits on terms that the developing countries cannot meet; insufficient attention to exports; and in some cases, excessive military purchases or financial mismanagement." So far so good. However, its conclusion by no means follws: "Whatever the causes, future export earnings of some countries are so heavily mortgaged as to endanger continuing imports, investment, and development. *All countries will have to address this problem together."* [36] But most of this debt is owed specifically to the United States, or is at least denominated in U.S. dollars (as is the case, for instance, of World Bank loans financed by dollar borrowings abroad). To call for all countries to help amoritze this U.S. dollar-debt is to ask for a net foreign exchange transfer from other developed nations (specifically Europe and Japan) to the United States. Foreign governments are thus being asked to realign their aid policies not only to stimulate the sale of U.S. goods (by untying their aid), but to help the United States recoup its political-economic investment in past, essentially bilateral aid.

The report rightly observes that "keeping these countries on a short leash by emergency debt rescheduling operations does not show the necessary foresight. Countries with serious debt problems, in trying to avoid default, are likely to impose more internal and exchange restrictions and thereby intensify their future difficulties." [37] But it effectively insists that they indeed be kept on a leash, and that any given country's debt be rescheduled only if it demonstates" by its plans and policies that it is pursuing a coherent development program of appropriate fiscal and financial policies." These policies consist of deflation at home and a dismantling of any protectionist trade and monetary policies which the country might have enacted. Such countries must open their economies to foreign trade and investment and "show determination to develop" by employing population control.

The commission seeks to prevent the African countries from accepting associate membership in the Common Market, by insisting that the United States retaliate by offering special tariff preferences to Latin America, thereby freezing Africa out of the United States market. [38]

The report does recognize, however, that it would be too much to expect Europe to subscribe to the Inter-American Development Bank (IDB) or to participate in concessional lending to the more backward Latin American countries, for there would be really little to gain in such a program. The IDB, concludes, will thus have to continue being funded by the United States, although it may well continue to borrow in Canada, Europe and Japan (thereby using its aid-apparatus to help finance the United States payments deficit, by transforming liquid available foreign-held dollars into a demand for United States exports of goods and services to its aid-clients rather than into potential claims on the country's gold stock).

*4. The Struggle against the Social Revolution Abroad.* The Peterson Report recommends that social revolution and protectionist tendencies abroad be staved off by (a) free trade policies and an open international investment climate, (b) an increasing proportion of local manpower allocated to the armed forces for domestic and foreign policing operations, (c) introduction of modern, capital-intensive technology, particularly in agriculture, even where this tends to displace the peasants from their lands and contributes to the rural exodus, and (d) mass population control so as to alleviate economic pressures on existing social institutional constraints.

The report sets out by repeating the obsolete endorsements of free trade, asserting that laissez faire policies add "to the real incomes of all participating countries and help to contain inflationary pressures. Of course, they also might result in adjustment problems. But, difficult as such adjustment problems sometimes are, they are temporary." This latter assertion depends on whether a quarter-or half-century is considered temporary. For when the opportunity-costs of pursuing free trade are added into the equation--a practice which the cross-section analysis of neo-classical economics does not condone—then real incomes in the less efficient economies over the longer term are in considerable danger of being reduced by the pursuit of laissez faire policies. This was emphasized by United States protectionists in the 1850's, who urged their country to adopt protectionism in order to insulate its producers from those of Europe, and to foster an "uneconomic" industry rather than to remain an agricultural, rural, slave-holding, raw-material exporting country.

The usual austerity programs are endorsed by the commission: "Checking the pace of inflation and introducing more realistic exchange rates helped achieve an economic turnaround in Brazil and Argentina [N.B: and also the revolutions which overthrew both governments] , and an increased reliance on market incentives was essential to the success of the 'Green Revolution' in India and Pakistan and to the diversification of Colombia's exports."[39] One wonders (but doubts) whether the Green Revolution in India and Pakistan refers to the recent spate of rural uprisings in India by peasants claiming that they were being displaced from their land by subsidized technology. The report euphemistically calls for the aid-borrowing countries to pay off their debts to the United States Treasury by inviting United States firms to accelerate their participation in their export sectors: "Developing countries cannot be expected to reach the point of financing their own development unless they are given the opportunity to earn the means for doing so through an increase in their exports." Towards this goal of fostering attractive export-sector investment opportunities the report endorses regional free-trade areas, but not political integration.

The Peterson Commission's motivation for endorsing population control will be dealt with in Section III below, following a review of the Pearson Commission's similar recommendations to the World Bank.

# II
## a dissenting view
## of the world bank

Elsewhere[40] I have described how the World Bank and IMF were established under the aegis of United States diplomats in 1944 to serve United States self-interest as it evolved in the years following World War II. During 1946-52 the World Bank played a major role in helping Europe reconstruct its war-torn economy, providing it with some $0.7 billion in loans (amounting to half its lending during these years). Then, during 1952-68 it turned to the backward countries, financing some $9.8 billion of exports from the industrial center (about one third of which came from the United States).

Had this been the sole extent of its operations it would have served the interests of both developed and backward countries alike. However, many aspects of its loan program militated against the development of the aid-borrowing countries. Its loans tended to be for industry rather than for agriculture, for the export sector rather than the domestic sector. They were extended to governments rather than to the private sector, and therefore (in these years) to institutions of the status quo rather than those of social-economic change. Partly becuase of these built-in biases the effect of Bank lending was to aggravate the food deficit rather than to help overcome it, and to centralize the role of existing federal governments.

By 1968 the Bank's future in fact looked cloudy. The aid-borrowing countries had reached the limits of their credit-worthiness. They could not afford to submit to any more aid on traditional hard terms. They were obliged to repay interest and principal on past aid out of deteriorating net balances on their commercial trade and services. Most of these countries had virtually reached the limit of their ability to borrow foreign currencies on hard commercial terms: their annual debt-servicing costs amounted to $4.7 billion by 1968, a sum equal to about 20% of their aggregate export earnings on goods and services (vs. only 10% at the outset of the 1960's and twice the amount of their new grants and loans.[41]

In order to refinance their outstanding indebtedness to maintain their solvency, they were forced to redirect their economies so as to sacrifice domestic growth to tightening balance-of-payments contraints. The result was a misshapen growth pattern that weakened even further their long-term position. They seemed to be falling further and further behind the developed nations.

In April 1968 President Johnson named Secretary of Defense Robert McNamara to succeed George Woods as president of the World Bank. Mr. McNamara was not the first president of the World Bank to come from the Pentagon. John J. McClory (1947-49) was Assistant Secretary of War. Mr. McNamara is, however, the first non-banker to head the agency.[42] Some observers must have found his appointment to be ironic, coming as he did from a previous service in which his major achievement was not to build but to destroy (most specifically, the economy of Vietnam). At any rate, his first act as incoming head of the bank was inauspiciously to help finance (albeit somewhat indirectly) the Vietnam War. He borrowed some $1.2 billion during his first year in office--three times the 1966/67 pace--of which some $0.4 billion took the form of dollar-borrowings in Europe, which were then invested in United States Treasury bills, government agency securities, and United States banks--thereby contributing this sum to the United States balance of payments (as measured on the "official transactions basis"). Another $0.2 billion (followed by a sharp acceleration to $0.5 billion in 1969) was transferred to the United States economy as a byproduct of normal World Bank financed purchases of capital goods ($140 million) and services ($35 million).[43] This $0.6 billion inflow offset some 15% of the foreign-exchange costs of United States overseas military spending during 1969. Because this military account was the major net source of disequilibrium in the United States payments deficit, any transactions working to supply United States payments inflows served to "finance" this section's net imbalance. Thus, World Bank operations during Mr. McNamara's first year in office served in large part to finance the operations of the United States military establishment which he had just left. In fact, he took it upon himself to announce, in his maiden speech as incoming president of the Bank, that a new function of its operations would henceforth be to transfer funds from payment-surplus to payments-deficit countries (that is, from Europe to the United States). And not a word of protest from Europe!

Mr. McNamara's appointment may best be viewed as an extension of his authority as ideological strategist of Pax Americana from national to world scope. Having supervised the revamping of the Pentagon's role in America's society and that of its allies, he was elevated to a position as guiding head of the world's major development lending institution. He was now able to lay down explicit social policy conditions to be adopted by all

TABLE 3

Estimated IBRD effects on U.S. balance of payments
from inception of IBRD through calendar year 1969

(In millions of U.S. dollars)

| | Inception to 12/31/59 | 1960 | 1961 |
|---|---|---|---|
| U.S. Payment of 1 percent subscription | $ 64 | $ - | $ - |
| U.S. Payment of 9 percent subscription | 571 | - | - |
| IBRD bonds sold in United States, net of redemptions | 957 | 32 | 41 |
| Net IBRD loan sales in United States | 146 | 44 | 2 |
| Investment income earned by IBRD in United States | 137 | 42 | 42 |
| | 1,875 | 118 | 85 |
| IBRD-financed goods bought in United States 1/ | 1,783 | 148 | 136 |
| Interest paid by IBRD to U.S. bondholders | 187 | 38 | 40 |
| Interest paid by IBRD borrowers to U.S. loan holders | 28 | 7 | 12 |
| IBRD administrative expenses in United States (including bond issuance cost) | 84 | 10 | 11 |
| Total paid by IBRD to United States | 2,082 | 203 | 199 |
| Net paid by IBRD to United States | 207 | 85 | 144 |
| IBRD-Long-Term Investments in United States | - | - | - |
| Net paid by IBRD to United States and | $207 | $ 85 | $ 114 |

1. Includes procurement specifically identifiable as originating in the
   United States and the same proportion of procurement not identifiable
   by country of origin

2. Maturities over one year.

| | | Calendar Year | | | | | | Inception to 12/31/69 |
|---|---|---|---|---|---|---|---|---|
| 1962 | 1963 | 1964 | 1965 | 1966 | 1967 | 1968 | 1969 | 12/31/69 |
| $ - | $ - | $ - | $ - | $ - | $ - | $ - | $ - | $ 64 |
| - | - | - | - | - | - | - | - | 571 |
| 68 | -19 | -40 | 141 | 6 | 187 | 213 | 64 | 1,650 |
| 79 | 76 | 22 | -35 | -50 | -55 | -27 | -44 | 158 |
| 54 | 54 | 51 | 54 | 54 | 56 | 59 | 92 | 695 |
| 201 | 111 | 33 | 160 | 10 | 188 | 245 | 112 | 3,138 |
| 176 | 209 | 146 | 136 | 148 | 147 | 140 | 110 | 3,279 |
| 42 | 42 | 43 | 45 | 50 | 58 | 72 | 87 | 704 |
| 12 | 14 | 17 | 17 | 16 | 13 | 11 | 9 | 156 |
| 13 | 15 | 17 | 22 | 27 | 29 | 36 | 40 | 304 |
| 243 | 280 | 223 | 220 | 241 | 247 | 259 | 246 | 4,443 |
| 42 | 169 | 190 | 60 | 231 | 59 | 14 | 134 | 1,305 |
| - | - | - | 240 | 341 | 179 | 161 | 382 | 1,303 |
| $ 42 | $ 169 | $ 190 | $ 300 | $ 572 | $ 238 | $ 175 | $ 156 | $2,608 |

Controller's Department
Accounting Division
February 6, 1970

applicants for World Bank loans. To assert that he personally proceeded to transform the World Bank's operating philosophy into a vehicle for American Cold War aims is not at all to put forth a merely *ad hominem* argument. For in view of the dovetailing of World Bank operations into Pax Americana strategy since he took office, and in light of the convergence of views between the Peterson and Pearson Commissions, the question must inevitably arise as to whether his appointment merely epitomizes the subversion of World Bank operations to United States Cold War policies for the 1970's. For just as under Mr. McNamara's regime as Secretary of Defense foreign aid became increasingly military or para-military in nature, being used more and more to prop up the status quo of politically friendly governments, so the resources of the World Bank were mobilized to serve as a vehicle for militant United States policy abroad.

This is not to deny that Mr. McNamara faced very real institutional problems upon joining the Bank. For instance it was clear that he was taking over an institution that could not long continue to expand its lending under the constraints imposed by its 1944 Articles of Agreement. For one thing, it was permitted to lend only for self-amortizing projects, that is, for projects which would generate a direct earnings flow (and/or foreign exchange gain, either by generating exports or by displacing imports) sufficient to amortize the bank's loan and pay its interest charges. Few such projects were available, as an increasing proportion of the aid-borrowing countries' balance-of-payments inflows was earmarked for the repayment of past borrowings. Their creditworthiness declined accordingly.

Furthermore, whereas the Bank had been able to borrow long-term funds at 2%-3% in the early years of its lending, by 1968 it found itself obliged to pay nearly 7%, thereby burdening the backward countries with interest charges nearly three times as high as those of the 1940's. As the same time that these countries found their debt-servicing costs increasing, they also generally found their net balance-of-payments positions deteriorating, as their almost universal attempt to achieve an industrial revolution without a simultaneous agricultural revolution had resulted in declining food output per capita, an accelerating rural exodus and a mounting food deficit. The more they borrowed to industrialize the further their trade account deteriorated and the smaller their ability to attract further foreign borrowings became.

Already in 1963, the year in which Mr. McNamara's predecessor George Woods took over the Bank's helm, it was recognized that there was a scarcity of projects qualifying for investment on the Bank's hard-loan terms. This led Mr. Woods to press for supplementary financing for the Bank's soft-loan affiliate, the International Development Association (IDA). Nonetheless, the Bank's members elected not to provide IDA with the additional funds requested. This was largely the result of growing disillusion already at this time with existing aid institutions and policies, an understandable reaction in view of the deteriorating economic position of the aid-borrowing countries, coupled with the reluctance of most of their governments to take political-economic steps to reverse this trend. In recognition of this governmental inertia, Mr. McNamara observed, in his speech to the Bank's September 1968 annual meeting which set forth his new policies, that "blatant mismanagement of economies; diversion of scarce resources to wars of nationalsim; perpetuation of discriminatory systems of social behavior and income distribution have been all too common in these countries. . . .But it is equally clear that the political will to foster development has weakened, is weakening further and needs desperately to be strengthened." The backward countries--or more particularly, their governments--had painted themselves into a corner from which they needed extraordinary help to escape.

Faced with these problems Mr. McNamara effected a fundamental policy change in Bank operations. Without explicitly calling attention to the fact, he renounced Article IV, Sec. 10 of the Bank's charter, which prohibited it from exerting political pressure upon member nations to alter their social institutions, and the article obligating it to make loans "for productive [i.e., financially self-amortizing] purposes" only.

Article IV had been intended to prevent the kind of conflict of interest between lender and borrower that inevitably characterizes bilateral intergovernmental lending. As discussed in the previous section, such loans are generally granted in exchange for political or military favors which may or may not be in the long-term interests of the borrowing country. Mr. McNamara correctly perceived, however, that it was precisely the Bank's inability to lay down social-political preconditions for its loans that had been a major factor in the disappointing results of its lending to the backward countries: it had been obliged to work within the political-economic context of their status quo.

The hard loan provision had been designed to avoid squandering funds on merely showcase projects, by requiring each project stand on its own financial feet. The effect of this project-by-project approach, however, was to force the Bank into a somewhat narrow view of economic development: only the immediate internal economies of projects under consideration were weighed, rather than the external economies so vital in true development lending. The Bank's move towards viewing the overall financial effects of its lending (such as, for instance, in its mass birth control programs), and towards program lending in general thus represented a tendency towards a more dynamic evaluation of the effects of its loan projects–in economic jargon, a transition from partial equilibrium to general equilibrium analysis.

Both these policy changes were potentially salutary. Indeed, dropping the two constraints in question fundamentally broadened the scope of World Bank operations as it prepared to enter the 1970's. Unfortunately, Mr. McNamara chose as his designated vehicle through which to introduce these policy changes a neo-Malthusian policy of mass population control: the Bank's first course, he announced, would be "to let the developing nations know the extent to which rapid population slows down their potential development, and that, in consequence, the optimum employment of the world's scarce development funds requires attention to this problem" In this statement he declared his intention to use Bank funds as a political lever to induce mass population control in borrowing countries, even where this policy is not endorsed by their governments (especially those of Roman Catholic Latin America). Secondly, he indicated his intent to make loans for projects which are not in themselves directly self-amortizing, for the returns from birth control are indirect at best.

Although he observed that outmoded social institutions represent a check to the expansion of food output needed to sustain population growth in the backward countries at current rates he did not go so far as to advocate that these institutions be transformed, particularly those concerning land tenure. Instead, he advocated simply that population growth be curtailed to match that modest rate of gain in food output which existing institutional constraints would permit, thereby implicitly endorsing these constraints as inherent political-institutional checks to the growth of population.

Mr. McNamara's speech was widely popularized in the Anglo-Saxon nations, although it was generally received with misgivings in Roman Catholic countries and in the more race-conscious non-white nations.[44] The upshot has been to usher in a long-needed debate as to the assumptions and values of economic development. In this debate Mr. McNamara has seized the initiative: to provide doctrinal defense for his policies he appointed Canada's ex-Prime

Minister Lester Pearson in August 1968 to head a Bank-financed commission whose conclusions, he correctly anticipated, would endorse its neo-Malthusianism. The commission's report, *Partners in Development,* was published one year later.

In the words of the *Washington Post* review of October 5, "It reads like ...well, like a long report. ...an establishment pronouncement, not a maverick critique ...bypassing questions of the desirability or unavoidability of radical political and social change." It endorses the palliatives of population control and transplanted technology to buy some more time in which to fend off the social-economic transformation so urgently called for in the backward countries. Its analysis is static and asocial, pinioned narrowly within its Malthusian mantle. It presupposes that the backward countries have a natural and permanent competitive disadvantage in food production, so that they are implicitly held to be competitors neither in manufactures nor in food. They seem left with only foreign-financed, capital-intensive mining and petroleum investments with which to finance their economic growth. The great bulk of their population is thus doomed to lives of underemployed irrelevance. Hence the need for mass population control.

One is struck by the report's exclusively technological usage of the term "revolution." There is a Green Revolution (pp. 49, 61), which turns out to be the introduction of new seed varieties, fertilizers and irrigation pumps to create a highly capitalized agribusiness enclave, rather than peasant uprisings. There is an Industrial Revolution (p. 5), and indeed the report erroneously attributes the origin of modern economic development to the Industrial Revolution which began in England "some two hundred years ago," rather than to the agricultural transformations of the sixteenth century which formed the preconditions for modern industrial growth. There are assorted references to revolutions in transport and communications, medicine and other aspects of the "technological revolution." But there is no reference anywhere to *revolution* in its political-social context. For this, various euphemisms are employed.

The *Century Dictionary and Cyclopaedia* provides some pertinent definitions for the word *revolution* as used in the Pearson report: "1. The act of revolving or turning completely round, so as to bring every point of the turning body back to its first position. 2. The act of moving completely around a circular or oval course, independently of any revolution. In a revolution without rotation, every part of the body moves by an equal amount..." This is really excellent! A revolution without rotation (that is, without social change) is what is after all being proposed by the World Bank today, a technological revolution as a kind of *deus ex machina* in which "every part of the body moves by an equal amount," that is, where social relations remain unchanged. Growth is to be scalar rather than structural, evolutionary, or developmental. The technological revolution, including the medical wonders of birth control, may be mobilized to stave off any revolution of a non-technological nature.

The most immediate economic problem in the backward countries is that their food output has fallen behind their population growth. Indeed, they may be characterized as backward more in the agricultural than in the industrial sense, for until they undergo an agricultural revolution such as that which freed the expansive forces of capitalism in England, Germany, France, etc., they cannot expect to build a base on which to industrialize. Given the fact that their population growth is outpacing their food output, necessitating a growing volume of imports and thus becoming a primary factor in their chronic balance-of-payments deficits, the solution must be either of two alternatives: (a) they may reduce their rate of population growth to match that of their inadequate food production--that is, to meet the constraints of their archaic forms of land tenure and associated agricultural backwardness, or (b) they may increase their food output to keep pace with their population growth through a process of agricultural modernization– while working to increase per capita earnings in the expectation that as incomes increase the rate of population growth will decrease (a relationship that has been demonstrated for centuries in virtually every country of the world).

Policy *(a)* is conservative, intended specifically to conserve the institutions of backwardness. Policy *(b)* sets out to repeat in the agriculturally backward countries the creation of an owner-operated farm sector upon which an industrial base may ultimately thrive, finding in it both a home market and a steady supply of labor.

Unfortunately, the Pearson Report endorses Mr. McNamara's neo-Malthusian heresy: it calls for mass population control measures to curtail demographic growth in the backward countries, prescribing that modest rate of gain which their archaic agricultural institutions can sustain. In order to maintain the integrity of these outmoded institutions it calls for a Green Revolution, in the vain hope that an isolated agribusiness sector may be created to keep the unproductive population at least well-fed (and presumably content). Should these most modern farm techniques be successfully transplanted within the georgraphic borders of the agriculturally backward countries, as little as 10-20 percent of the population might feed the remaining mouths. As a purely engineering problem, this is technologically possible. However, what is *not* touched upon in the report is the mass rural unemployment that would follow from this new enclave of modernity. Will it become a massive rural exodus of untrained, unemployable labor (as it has become even in developed nations such as the United States), burdening the cities with an unmanageable social overhead? Is it to be left on the land to eke out subsistence livelihood on meager plots? Because the 400-page report's discussion is couched only in aggregate terms of "national" food output relative to "national" population (class structures and their problems not being acknowledged), these structural problems are not recognized.

Indeed, the report nowhere advocates a transformation of the institutions of rural backwardness: the Green Revolution is not social but purely technological. Population control and transplanted technology are put forth as *alternatives* to social modernization: only by curtailing population growth in the backward countries can the existing institutions of land tenure be sustained in the face of those truly revolutionary pressures which swept them away in Europe centuries ago.

The report proposes a ten-point program:

1. *To create a framework for free and equitable international trade.* Free trade is essentially a doctrine of the status quo. Its workings tend to perpetuate existing patterns of comparative advantage and disadvantage among nations. Thus, in advocating free trade the Pearson Report (like the Peterson Report) would prevent the backward countries from shaping their own development. They may not insulate their comparatively low productivity economies from the existing international market forces which must necessarily swamp their domestic producers in the absence or commercial barriers.

2. *To promote mutually beneficial flows of foreign private investment.* Aid-recipient countries must provide a "general climate for private activity. Disincentives to such activity should be identified and removed wherever consistent with legitimate national goals." In other words, the main growth-sectors of these countries must be permitted to fall into foreign hands, inevitably contributing to the chronic payments deficits which stifle their development over the longer term. Presumably, anti-trust regula-

tion would not be a "legitimate national goal" if applied by a less developed country. Presumably, their economies are to be cartellized in a manner prohibited in the more advanced nations.

Reviewing the report, Charles Elliott has observed that it "rightly urges that the auction that has developed for foreign private funds is not in the best interests of the developing countries themselves (though it misses the important analytical point that such incentives distort the choice of technologies in the direction of capital intensity), but does not see that this auction has developed precisely because some developing countries find that they need a constantly increasing inflow of foreign funds to offset the outflow resulting from the repatriation of profits generated by already existing foreign capital."[45] This foreign-exchange outflow is also imposed by the aid-recipients' debt-service charges on past aid-borrowing. Given today's ground rules of international finance, foreign aid-lending leads inexorably to a loss of commercial autonomy by the less developed countries, and to their resources consequently being turned over to foreign ownership.

3. *To establish a better partnership, a clearer purpose, and a greater coherence in development aid.* Partners in what: in progress or backwardness? And on whose terms? On these touchy points the report is discretely silent. In Elliot's words, "there is very little suggestion in the report that aid can in fact be obstructive to development and even growth. . . .Even in the discussion of food aid it is hard to perceive that the Commission has considered seriously the mounting volume of evidence that food aid has acted as a real constraint on the development of agriculture in the food deficit countries. While the report seeks to explode the myth that aid has been wasteful in the sense of misappropriated or mis-applied, it comes nowhere near to discussing the way it has been used as a political tool to keep in power obstructive and regressive regimes, particularly in Latin America."[46]

4. *To increase the volume of aid.* The world is now rich enough to afford the economic slavery of entire nations whose archaic institutions are supported by donations from the wealthier countries. The report recommends 1% of the "wealthier nations'" GNP be "given" (i.e., lent) abroad, as if the issue were merely one of income distribution rather than differential productive abilities. The Pearson Commission apparently feels no twinge of embarrassment at using the term "aid" throughout the report with no qualifying quotation marks around it. But aid, as defined by it, is far from being any net economic burden for the developed countries: military assistance, export promotion and administrative

overhead are all lumped together in the "aid"-barrel.

5. *To meet the problem of mounting debts.* These debts are caused in large part by past aid-borrowings and the misshapen profiles of development they have helped foster. The report does *not* advocate a moratorium on these debts, that is, to transform past governmental investment into current true aid. It is no more ready to see these debts wiped off the books than the United States government would agree in 1931 to abolishing the Inter-Allied World War I debts. Instead, it proposes to constrain future economic evolution in the backward countries by their existing debt burden, and indeed to make this burden heavier: "If future debt crises are to be forestalled, *sound financial policies* must be pursued and the terms of aid must be lenient."(Italics added.) By this the commission means that deflationary monetary policies must be imposed on countries suffering heavy debt burdens, although such a policy would stifle their ability to use expansionary monetary policies to finance domestic growth.

The "stabilization" plans recommended by the IMF World Bank missions to Argentina and Turkey in 1958 contributed to the fall of both governments, and usually represent a source of national discontent wherever applied, as they place international payments balance over domestic equilibrium. Any knowledgeable reader must be struck by the sharp contrast between the commission's call for balance-of-payments equilibrium in the less developed countries, while governments in the industrial nations, particularly the United States, are deliberately pursuing full employment policies without respect to the massive payments deficits which follow.

6. *To make aid administration more effective.* Although the commission's recommendation that aid be "untied" is to be applauded, it is hardly likely that it will be taken to heart by the United States--although the United States would of course benefit from other nations untying *their* aid. For if the United States proceeded to untie its aid, the result would be a sharp deterioration in its balance of payments which could not be sustained (and which, we can imagine, would soon be followed in short order by a reduction in its foreign-aid program). This seems to be one of the commission's dead letter recommendations.

In fact, the degree to which the United States is proceeding to tie even its aid to ostensibly multinational organizations such as the Asian Development Bank is curiously not receiving adequate publicity. For instance, the amended Asian Development Bank Act, Section 1, paragraph 1, sec. 13 (c) (1) provides that all of the

$100 million United States contribution to the Bank's "Special Fund"—that is, its soft-loan window—be tied: "The United States Special Resources may be expended by the Bank only for procurement in the United States of goods produced in, or services supplied from, the United States, except that the United States Governor, in consultation with the National Advisory Council on International Monetary and Financial Policies, may allow eligibility for procurement in other member countries from the United States Special Resources if he determines that such procurement eligibility would materially improve the ability of the bank to carry out the objectives of its special finds resources and would be compatible with the international financial position of the United States." By way of contrast, the bill's sponsor (Rep. Reuss of Wisconsin) observes, "Several contributors to the special funds have already made their funds available for procurement in other member countries."[46a]

7. *To redirect technical assistance.* The report pays lip service to the fact that "strong institutional support" (i.e., social modernization) is requisite for technical assistance to have a positive effect, "particularly in the fields of agriculture and education." Its attempt to portray agricultural productivity as evolving rapidly under the impulse of modern technology is highly misleading, however. Not only does it ignore the problem of the rural exodus, but as Mr. Elliot observed, "by being sufficiently vague, because aggregative, the report can sound more optimistic than a disaggregated analysis of the facts would really justify. Another more alarming example is the way in which the 'green revolution' is described. All the figures quoted are from climatically good years and the comparisons are drawn with climatically bad years. Similarly, the report nowhere allows for inflation and can therefore make optimistic comparisons of *money* values in the future, ignoring *real* values." Mr. Elliot suspects the reason to be that "To have emphasized the pessimistic appreciation of the situation would merely have strenthened the disillusionment. . . . " [47] thereby impeding further implementation of the Bank's preferred neo-classical policies.

8. *To slow the growth of population.* Nations must follow Malthusian policies in order to qualify for future Bank loans: "Aid-givers cannot be indifferent to whether population problems recieve the attention they require, and both bilateral and international agencies should press for adequate analysis of these problems and their bearing on development programs. . . . In particular, social policies which reduce the dependence on the

family as the sole source of security would lessen the need and desire for large families." It seems that the backward countries must become welfare states: they must divert what net economic surplus they may produce from the production sphere towards the consuption sphere in a massive attempt to break the traditional family structures. "Social justice" programs permitted the backward countries are thus in sharp contrast to those pursued in developed nations such as the United States. For the backward countries, the prescribed retardation of demographic growth becomes a direct function of social backwardness: the less capable their institutions, the more they must cut back their population growth to "live with" these institutions.

9. *To revitalize aid to education and research.* This is a valid element of the Report's advocated strategy, but one which is unattainable within the confines of an open international economy. For education and research must be either self-financed by the private sector, or government financed. If the labor force or its employers are to finance education, then it must do so out of high wages. This requires protected industries, which in turn presupposes some form of blocism. If public education is to be financed a rapid increase in governmental expenditures is required which must be inflationary unless matched by similarly increased taxes—which would again add to the cost-structure of these countries and would therefore form some special tariff-protection. This financial quandery is not analyzed in the report.

10. *To strengthen the multilateral aid system,* by moving from bilateral aid to multilateral aid. The report does not acknowledge the degree to which allegedly multilateral institutions--the World Bank, IDA, IFC, and the IMF--are dominated by United States and British government appointees who steer their course to meet the dictates of American world strategy. One might at first sight, for instance, be tempted to laud the proposal that balance of-payments surplus countries transfer a given portion of their payments gain to the backward countries to ease their debt problems--up to, say, $5 billion per year in the form of Special Drawing Rights transfers, as has been proposed by United States monetary authorities. However, under the United States plan the main beneficiary of this income-transfer would be the United States: for SDR's are "created" by countries' payments deficits, mainly those of the United States and Britain. Thus, the foreign exchange resources of other developed nations—mainly Europe and Japan—would be transferred to Latin America and other less developed areas for them to repay mainly dollar borrowings and to purchase dollar

goods and services. A triangular flow would be set in motion from Eruope and Japan to the backward countries on "SDR-aid" account and then to the United States as remitted earnings and amor-tization on United States investments and past aid-lending. This would finance the United States payments deficit on government military and agency spending. It is thus ironically proposed to help the less developed countries by helping the United States finance its military-inspired deficit. The United States thus seeks the backward countries' allegiance in a move, as a united front, against the world's creditor nations. So long as it and Britain remain in substantial payments deficit, this form of "SDR-aid" is of questionable world utility.

# III
## political aspects of u.s.
## and world bank aid-doctrine

The above analysis goes far beyond merely demonstrating that the defects of World Bank and United States State Department aid policy have been the result simply of some ethnocentric, neo-classical, post-Keynesian or other innocently misguided philosophy of economic development. Such an interpretation would beg the question of how these unfortunate philosophies came to be adopted in the first place. They were, as we have seen, the deliberate product of unique United States Cold War aims, above all preservation of the international status quo.

The difficulty of supplanting outmoded aid- and development-doctrines with a more appropriate strategy therefore lies precisely in the fact that such a strategy does not happen to be that which maximizes today's United States Cold War gains. Development of a thriving Third World bloc seems to be at odds with the very philosophy of the United States nation-state. Thus, even though a more effective development philosophy may be formualted—as its outlines have already been—it seems doubtful that it could gain sponsorship by the Bank or by the State Department. Freeing the backward countries from their yoke of obsolete economic doctrines and social systems must therefore entail not only re-education but at some point direct political action.

The ultimate action, as will be discussed below, would be for them to withdraw from the World Bank, GATT and the IMF altogether and to form a new set of development institutions, to be run by themselves and in their own interests. For until such a set of institutions is inaugurated, they can benefit only indirectly from United States and European economic growth: they will be "aided" only to the extent that their growth patterns mesh into an increasingly rigidified United States self-interest. For these countries, continued capitulation to neo-classical "growth" doctrines offers little promise of substantial economic and social evolution.

Despite the fact that the World Bank is dominated mainly by United States self-interest, it may be argued, the question still remains as to whether or not the aid-borrowing countries should retain their membership on the ground that the net borrowing of *some* resources, even on less than optimal terms, is better than no resources at all. The answer of course depends on whether their economic development is on balance fostered or impaired by World Bank loan programs.

According to most economic models, *any* aid or capital import necessarily increases economic growth. The traditional neo-classical model, for instance, computes, a "capital-output" ratio (according to which the dollar-value of existing aggregate "capital" is balanced against dollar-GNP) and associates each average dollar of new "capital" (or aid) with X-dollars of added output. It hypothesizes that incremental foreign direct investments and aid-dollars contribute to GNP by a "multiplier" based on this national (average) capital-output ratio: if a nation's output is four times its existing capital resources, for instance, then each additional dollar of capital is expected to contribute $4 to its GNP. Two authors have recently published a study, however, which indicates that "the opposite hypothesis is closer to the truth: in general, foreign assistance is not associated with progress and, indeed, may deter it. If the growth which a nation achieves, or fails to achieve, is related to the assistance it receives, one finds that there is no support for the view that aid encourages growth. . .Taking the average rate of growth of GNP over the years 1957-64 for the twelve [Latin American] countries for which figures are available, we find that it is inversely related to the ratio of foreign aid to GNP."[48]

Why did this inverse correlation between economic growth and foreign aid inflows occur? One reason, the authors suggest, is that foreign resources may displace domestic investment rather than supplement it: foreign private capital tends to preempt the growth areas of the economy, while aid resources may reduce the urgency for governments to foster an investment climate to mobilize domestic resources. "Moreover, governments, finding abundant resources abroad, expand their consumption, too, and refrain from raising taxes. In other words, aid frequently becomes a substitute for tax reforms."[49]

The major adverse effect of foreign aid, however, is less direct. A usual diplomatic precondition for aid is that no move be taken towards protective insulation of the economy or related mobilization of domestic resources. "Perhaps the most important reason why foreign assistance frequently hinders growth is that it prevents. . . institutional changes. In part because the lending country may not accept the wisdom of such changes, in part because aid enables the borrowing country to postpone them, such reforms as changes in land tenure patterns are not instituted. Foreign aid tends to strengthen the status quo; it enables those in power to evade and avoid fundamental reforms; it does little more than patch plaster on the deteriorating social edifice."[50] Questions as to the validity of the State Department-World Bank strategy of economic development thus inevitably resolve themselves into those of a political nature, and concern above all the retarding effect of their loan programs on positive institutional reform.

For instance, although many of the backward countries emerged from World War II as net food exporters, their supluses have steadily diminished since that time, and have in many cases turned to deficit. It is precisely this declining agricultural self-sufficiency that classifies them as backward. Their diminishing per capita food production has elicited two polarities of response, one radical and the other Malthusian.

To many development planners it indicates that their attempt to achieve an industrial revolution without a simultaneous agricultural revolution has failed, and that attention must now be turned to the neglected agricultural sector. Undue emphasis upon industrialization has contributed to a rural exodus to the cities, rising urban food needs in the face of a declining rural labor base, and a widening balance-of-payments drain on food account which has been a major factor in impairing their credit-worthiness. According to this reading, the solution to declining agricultural self-sufficiency does not lie in further emphasis on mining, petroleum or industrial manufactures with which to earn the funds to purchase more food imports, but rather in a structural transformation of agriculture through methods similar to those employed so successfully in the United States over the past century: educational extension services to promote an evolving agricultural technology, rural credit banks and price support programs to finance it, subsidized (or at least regulated) transport and crop distribution services, and a general fostering of owner-operated farms. In most backward countries, unfortunately, such programs are not possible under existing patterns of land tenure and their related institutions. The appropriate path of action is thus to socially and economically transform the countryside. For only by breaking down the institutional impediments to a modernized agriculture (*not* necessarily agribusiness) can these countries hope to regain their lost agricultural self-sufficiency.

To State Department strategists, Mr. McNamara, Ford Foundation planners and an increasing portion of the academic community, by way of contrast, failure of the backward countries to provide for their increasing numbers foretells first and foremost a rising revolutionary pressure for social transformation–and all the potential "dangers" of economic isolationism which this entails. This school does not look directly at the cause of the declining self-sufficiency in food production, but simply at its existence as a *fait accompli.*

It seems that "nature" or "technology" are at fault, not man's institutions. Presuming existing trends in farm productivity to persist (rather than to be reversed, as in the foregoing strategy), the inevitable political effect must indeed be revolution at some point. "As Secretary of Defense," Mr. McNamara reminisced in his September 1968 speech, "I have observed, and spoken publicly about, the connection between world poverty and unstable relations among nations." But instead of advocating a transformation of the institutions responsible for this poverty, he advised that population growth must be curtailed *so as to sustain* the very institutions whose shortcomings he had just decried.

For a man in the position of heading the world's major development-lending agency, Mr. McNamara has been curiously silent about all aspects of socio-economic transformation save those of birth control and the "technological revolution." He has made no major remarks concerning the backward countries' archaic systems of land tenure, rural credit, crop distribution patterns, the structural inadequacy of existing educational and tax systems, or the many other socio-economic impediments to their agricultural evolution. By introducing population control as the unique area in which the Bank is to exert political pressure for "social change," Mr. McNamara has preempted it from involving itself in the economic modernization of these countries. The food problem, essentially a problem of backwardness, has been construed as a "population problem," with birth control and labor-displacing agribusiness technology proposed as lone palliatives, rather than as complementary parts of a broader strategy to transform the agriculturally backward economies.

The effect of such theorizing has been to virtually write the Bank and the U.S. foreign aid program out of a prospective role in pursuing new alternatives to economic backwardness. Their fatal shortcoming lies in their conviction that merely technological or financial inputs may suffice to foster growth in the absence of an institutional environment in which these inputs may be productively utilized. They are plagued by the view that the *effect* of poverty--a high rate of population growth--may be attacked without simultaneously attacking its *causes*--social backwardness and institutional rigidity. Their proposals are thus put forth as an alternative to social and economic modernization, not as a means towards this end. The ex-Secretary of Defense might have suggested, for instance, that needed social reforms should be nurtured and accelerated by a new international lending authority established for that specific purpose, or even by a transformed World Bank. He might have theorized that the tendency of population growth to decline with rising per capita income (and indeed, simply with the introduction of electricity in many areas) would itself tend to slow the rate of population growth once the path of social progress was set upon. That he did neither of these indicates the limited scope of his outlook.

## political motives
## for the resurgence of malthusianism

The espousal of neo-Malthusian doctrine, first in the U.S. foreign aid program and soon thereafter by the World Bank, has laid them open to the accusation that their motive for recommending population control rests on the same political grounds as those of Malthus in the days of Britain's poor law debates: essentially as a substitute for social modernization. Obviously, population growth entails social costs for the backward countries, just as in the developed nations. It is, however, only one part of a larger picture.

The motive for today's wave of neo-Malthusianism is probably nothing so crude as a struggle for raw material supplies, despite the Paley Report's fears on this count back in 1952. True, population growth and economic development abroad will require greater domestic utilization of the backward countries' raw materials, thereby cutting into their available export surplus. True, additions to the poorer countries populations represent consumers of the raw materials their nations now provide to the industrial aid-lending bloc. Nonetheless, in view of the vast potential mineral wealth contained in the sea, the development of new raw-materials substitutes, and the technological advances in extractive techniques which have so dramatically increased the yield of already-existing world reserves, it is unlikely that the obsolete nightmare of imminent raw material scarcity could by itself have motivated the bank to resurrect the Malthusian heresy. Economic development abroad clearly works to increase markets for the advanced nations' industrial exports, especially their capital-goods industries, in exchange for whose output they must still provide raw materials.

Nor is it likely that racism underlies the Bank's new policy, despite the fact that population growth among the non-white and non-Anglo-Saxon nations is substantially outstripping that of the nations which today hold the balance of international power.

Admittedly, growing populations in the poorer countries will give them a large voice in international affairs by the mere power of numbers--as perceived centuries ago by the mercantilists in viewing population as potential military inputs.[51]

A more likely explanation is simply that the Bank's neo-Malthusianism and its endorsement of the political and economic status quo--following a similar shift in American foreign aid patterns--is part of a general strategy to freeze today's balance of power among all nations, as well as among the political parties within these nations, so as to maintain American hegemony and that of its political allies in the backward countries. Whether or not this is or is not a conscious plan, the fact remains that Mr. McNamara has enuciated that (1) population growth under existing institutional constraints implies political change, and (2) the present social-economic institutions have not significantly evolved, and will not significantly evolve, at the hands of the present governments, so that (3) further population growth implies a change of government, probably to the benefit of parties less closely associated with the United States.

In order to place the Bank's neo-Malthusian heresy in its long-term social perspective, we may briefly review the social context of population theorizing since the days of Malthus. The essence of his theory was the hypothesis that laborers respond to rising incomes by increasing their family size (and therefore their current consumption expenses) rather than reinvesting this income to improve their own standard of life. Children came before self-advancement. This theory was termed by Ferdinand Lassalle the Iron Law of Wages, as it implied that the reason why wages *could not* permanently increase was because any increase in aggregate wage payments would soon be followed by more mouths to feed. Since the time that this theory was enunciated, of course, it has been demonstrated to be erroneous in virtually every country in the world: as incomes rise, population growth tends to decelerate rather than to accelerate (although there may now be an initial transition period of simultaneous increase in both income levels and fertility). Furthermore, new men are producers as well as consumers, and are subject to increasing returns as the increased size of their market permits greater specialization of labor, capital and land, and a more rapid introduction of new capital. Only in the socially and economically backward countries where laborers do not possess this alternative of self-investment in their own human capital do they choose to expend their added income on more children.

What originally gave great force to Malthusian doctrine, of course, was its integration with the Ricardian theory of diminishing returns to land. New men were indeed producers as well as consumers, the Ricardians conceded, but in the agricultural sector they were less efficient ones, as each new agricultural worker was forced to apply his labors to more distant or less productive soils. By the 1850's this theory had been controverted both by historical experience and by general recognition of the potential impact of soil nutrients: because of economies of scale, not only in industry and distribution but *particularly* in agriculture, each addition to man's population was--under democratic social conditions--more efficient than the last. The Ricardian theory of soil as possessing some limited, fixed, "original and indestructible" fertility, and its conclusions as to the evolution of food prices and land rent over time, were abandoned. Any failure of society to provide for its increasing numbers was therefore *not* technological in nature but political, and lay with man's social utilization of nature and his distribution of its products rather than with nature itself.

Although some writers continued to preach an impending doom to fall when man's agricultural output bumped against some hypothetical upper limit,[52] by the early decades of the twentieth century Malthusian doctrine had fallen into clear disfavor. Thus the eleventh edition of the *Encyclopaedia Britannica* observed in 1911 that his theories had achieved popularity more by virtue of their political function than through any substantial validity: "It can scarcely be doubted that the favour which was at once accorded to the views of Malthus in certain circles was due in part to an impression, very welcome to the higher ranks of society, that they tended to relieve the rich and powerful of responsibility for the condition of the working classes, by showing that the latter had chiefly themselves to blame, and not either the negligence of their superiors or the institutions of the country. The application of his doctrines, too, made by some of his successors had the effect of discouraging all active effort for social improvement."

Already in the mid-nineteenth century Edward Spencer and others had sought to explain the documented tendency of population growth to slow as incomes increased--just the opposite of Malthus's theory. "Misery," noted Thorold Rogers, "is a far more powerful incentive to population than a check to it, as Adam Smith saw, and Malthus did not."[53] So marked was the inverse correlation between income levels and fertility that by the 1920's and 1930's the major warnings of population scholars had come to concern *de*population rather than overpopulation. Some automatic stabilizing mechanism seemed to exist to level off man's demographic growth, just as his economic capacity to sustain this demographic expansion accellerated.

Not until the 1950's did Malthusianism begin to creep back into vogue. Its renewed popularity followed largely from the fact that medical discoveries had sharply extended life expectancies throughout the world, with their greatest impact in the poorer nations whose citizens had hitherto been plagued with the shortest lifespans. The result was that, as in the days of the Poor Laws, a class of men was nurtured which stood in excess of that number which society's institutions were able to provide with opportunities for productive employment. These excess laborers indeed represented consumers who were not producers. As a group they stirred feelings of resentment by those charged with their support. This latter and more fortunate group was composed of men who, through birth or by their own exertions, enjoyed the privilege of being able to generate a net surplus in production, and who resented the diversion of a part of this surplus to support the rural exodus which was burdening their cities.

The stage was thus set for a renewal of Malthusian attitudes. Today, the revived popularity of Malthusianism among the richer industrial nations (and among the richer classes of the backward countries) appears similar in inspiration to that in the days of the Poor Law detates—namely, its ability to relieve the rich nations (or the lax governments of the backward countries) of responsibility for poverty in the poorer countries "by showing that the latter had chiefly themselves to blame, and not either the negligence of their superiors [i.e., the richer aid-donor nations] or the institutions of the country." Pessimistic and stagnationist population doctrine today thus seems to absolve the richer nations from undertaking a path of far-reaching social reform in the world's food-deficit, aid-borrowing countries, particularly the reform of quasi-feudal of collectivist agricultural institutions.

The *Encyclopaedia Britannica* review cited above further observed that Thomas Chalmers, an early nineteenth-century economic moralist, " 'reviews *seriatim* and gravely sets aside all the schemes usually proposed for the amelioration of the economic condition of the people' on the ground that an increase of comfort will lead to an increase of numbers, and so the last state of things will be worse than the first." A parallel to Chalmers' forebodings occurs today as advances in life-extending medical techniques are being portrayed as the indirect agents of economic plague, augmenting the growing class of consumers who are not producers. Now the provision of a medical revolution without laying plans to bring about a social-economic revolution was indeed thoughtless. However, the proposal to curtail population growth as a belated palliative for failing to modernize the backward countries' social and agricultural institutions–and essentially as a substitute for this modernization–is evil: it does not serve the needs of the backward countries, but rather the narrow short-term political interest of the aid-donor nations, specifically the United States, in maintaining this unsatisfactory status quo.

So long as demographic control continues to be conceived as a substitute for institutional reform we are dealing primarily with social and political motives rather than with the issue of population growth per se. It is not only these supra-economic motives that must be brought into uestion, hoever, but the issue as to whether population control along the lines evisioned by the Bank will in fact work. Can programmed population control, in short, be expected to "cure" poverty?

The answer seems negative. Because high rates of population growth are to a great extent the *result* of poverty, whether in the backward countries or in the poverty-pockets of the industrial nations, the basic impetus to population growth will be left untouched. This is not to say that rapid population does not make the task of economic evolution more difficult by increasing the social overhead and educational facilities necessary to nurture this population in the modern industrial world--but merely that it is essentially a secondary effect of backwardness rather than the primary cause. Not only does the rate of population growth tend to be inversely correlated with income, so that it will tend to become self-euilibrating as economic growth accelerates among the backward countries, but population control without fundamental social reform does nothing in itself to tackle the related underlying cuases of poverty. Its result can therefore only be an intensification of the vicious circle of economic poverty and social backwardness.

## conclusions

U.S. self-interest following World War II led the country's diplomats and aid-planners to defend only those types of "aid" which dovetailed into its Cold War military and commercial strategy. Only that form of growth abroad was promoted which integrated the backward countries into the developed nations' economic orbit. A ready-made, altruistic rationalization for this strategy was found in neo-classical analysis: its narrow emphasis on short-term maximization of "output" (GNP) rather than long-term growth indicated that the more developed nations (those with a comparative international advantage in industry and agribusiness) should accelerate their factory and farm exports, while obtaining their fuels and raw materials from the backward countries. For in effect food has become an industrial, capital-intensive commodity. The international division of labor was therefore endorsed as between "hewers of wood and drawers of water" (but no longer growers of food) on the one hand, and manufactories of the world and businessmen of the farm on the other. Neo-classical analysis further met U.S. policy-needs by calling for the backward countries to concentrate on their "high productivity" sectors (those with high capital-output ratios). At the head of this list stood their export industry, followed by their domestic manufacturing (generally foreign-controlled). Agriculture was neglected. Exploitation of raw material resources was emphasized rather than the accumulation of "sunk costs" in the form of labor and soil capital resources. The farm sector was sacrificed to industry and mining, which remain in large part foreign-owned. And in a futile attempt to keep urban food costs (hence wages) low, agricultural prices were kept at minimum levels through price controls, thereby stifling farm income and capital accumulation for the majority of these countries' farmers.

Unfortunately, whereas neo-classical doctrine had forecast that these countries' export industries would serve as their lead-sector, they turned out to be retarding once their indirect economic effects were taken into account. This is because true economic growth is not a disaggregated combination of various sectors' output, but an integral process which, (when successful) gradually invests labor and land with sunk capital: educational working skills for the labor force, and soil capital for the land. Economic expansion that is not accompanied by this accumulation of human and soil capital serves only to deplete society's resources by rendering them obsolescent. Economic progrsss if forestalled rather than fostered.

### the political economy of foreign aid

Under such conditions, when capital does come to be applied to agriculture on a large scale in these countries, it is mainly a form imported from an alien economy and unsuited for the particular stage of evolution at which these countries find their rural land and human resources. The result is that it displaces increasing numbers of men from the land, channelling them into the cities in search of urban employments. However, unlike the experience of England during the eighteenth and nineteenth centuries, these modern-day rural migrants do not qualify for urban work: whereas two hundred years ago all they needed were "hands" to power the relatively crude tools of the early Industrial Revolution, what is needed today is brains to operate modern sophisticated capital. Today's displaced peasants lack these modern skills, as they have never been given opportunity to develop the entrepreneurial senses which their counterparts in developed nations enjoyed in the bygone days of *their* early rural exodus. Thus, the backward countries find themselves torn between excessive population on the one hand and insufficient supplies of skilled labor on the other: they are population-rich and labor-scarce.

Importation of modern technology cannot in itself solve this problem. It may aid the already developed nations by stimulating their exports. In (neo-classical) theory it will *appear* to aid the backward countries, by seeming to offer a "Green Revolution" as an alternative to some more political form of revolution. But in the long run it will fail: it will create in the backward countries just that situation which it is designed to prevent: namely, mass unemployment and revolutionary discontent. Palliatives designed to ameliorate this discontent, such as population control to remove some of the pressure from these countries' "resources," will not work. For institutions rather than the more material resources of neoclassical economics are the major constraining factors at work. U.S. aid-diplomats have mistaken a theory of technology for one of political economy. Economics being a social science, however, the search for some truth existing beyond the confines of historical time and its social-institutional context is bound to be deceptive.

Not only the coil and pill but rising incomes as well seem necessary to bring about the reduction in fertility so ardently desired by population planners. But a precondition for these rising incomes is just that social and political transformation which the neo-Malthusians fear, and which their doctrines have for nearly two centuries been put forth to forestall. In this lies their quandery.

For these reasons the precepts of neo-classical economics are futile. High productivity (that is, high output-per-manhour) is

131

irrelevant to the backward countries as a normative criterion for allocating their resources and directing their growth. Today, what is needed is a sense of history more than of technology. Unfortunately, this historical approach is not promulgated by the World Bank group, as it implies a development strategy at odds with that desired by the United States and its allied aid-lending nations. For it is hardly in these nations' interest to see the institutions of today's international status quo altered in the direction of regional protectionism for the aid-borrowing countries.

As a result, these countries face a bias of aid-lending "development" strategy in favor more of regression than development. The aid which is offered tends to further unbalance their economies and stifle agricultural self-sufficiency, rather than to foster self-sustaining capital formation and balance-of-payments equilibrium. Finding themselves in such a situation, as we have remarked above, they have these choices of action: (1) they may remain memers of the Bank and suppliants to the U.S. State Department, so as to obtain *some* resources for *some* projects which might be valuable in themselves; (2) they may withdraw from the aid program altogether (that is, from the World Bank and the U.S. and other countries' bilateral aid-programs), which would essentially be a political act designed to demonstrate their intention to commit themselves to a more nationally-oriented development strategy; and finally (3) they may seek to reform the Bank from within, along with the aid-lending nations' bilateral loan programs.

To remain members of the World Bank Group is tantalizingly dangerous. For in order to qualify for new lending they must now design their entire development *philosophy* along Bank-endorsed lines--that is, along the lines of Malthusian technocracy. Project lending has given way to program lending, deliberately so as to magnify the strategic effect of Bank lending. Borrowing countries cannot really expect to "fool" the Bank by taking only that which it may offer while basically pursuing their own chosen path, for all future aid is to be conditional upon their implementing the Bank's overall stagnationist philosophy. .

To remain merely *pro forma* members of the Bank and its allied organizations such as the IMF and GATT would seem wasteful. At least by withdrawing they might recoup their original entry-costs, as well as taking a political and diplomatic step whose repercussions would be felt around the world. To be sure, it does not really seem probable that most of the backward countries are about to withdraw from the Bank. Such a decision must ultimately be made by national governments rather than "nations," and governments as the natural agents of the status quo tend to share the Bank's reticence to commit themselves to fundamental institutional modernization--although the recent experience of Peru gives hope that this inertia may now be changing. If the aid-borrowing countries do remain members of the Bank, however, it is to be hoped that they will seek to transform it from within. Foremost among the needed changes in its Articles of Agreement are:

1. To take its administration and development planning out of the hands of United States diplomats and their appointees, and certainly out of Washington, D.C. as a minimum initial symbolic step;

2. to terminate the use of Bank and IMF operations as a mechanism for helping to finance the United States payments deficit, particularly so long as this deficit follows mainly from the war in Southwest Asia; and

3. to set forth a new philosophy of development to supplant the neo-classical doctrines now endorsed by the World Bank, the post-Keynesian "stabilization" doctrines imposed by the IMF, and the free trade policies implemented by GATT.

If a new international lending organization is to be formed, it must certainly not be burdened with the restrictions against lending for agricultural development which characterize the World Bank. Indeed, its explicit function should be to finance agricultural transformation in the food-deficit nations.[54] A counterpart to the Bank's Economic Development Institute will be established from which a more dynamic and production-oriented doctrine of economic development may be braodcast. Need for such an educational center is all the more urgent in view of the World Bank's planned recruiting drive of personnel from the world's food-deficit countries. It would be tragic indeed if men who seek to solve the problems of their countries' development ohould fall heir to the stagnationist doctrines being promulgated by today's neo-Malthusians.

Such a transformation will be difficult. The State Department's and Bank's neo-Malthusian strategy is the product of their narrow social outlook, their irrational fear of change abroad, their suspicion that the growth of foreign economic capability may entail an economic and military threat to the United States and its fellow aid-lenders, and above all their over-weaning commitment to the status quo in the backward countries. Modern farm technology and birth control, the two central policies advocated by World Bank and State Department development theorists, are now

133

playing a fundamentally anti-social role in backward areas, as today's aid-technocrats are attempting to resolve these countries' food problem without the agency of these social changes which have characterized the agricultural revolutions in all of today's industrial nations. The aid-lending bloc's tragic shortcoming lies in its vain search for a technological solution to what is a social rather than a merely technological problem.

Mass availability and utilization of birth control is obviously a desirable alternative to today's multiplication of poverty. However, let it not be Malthusian and anti-social in its motive, but social: let it be a complement to economic modernization, not a substitute. For the essence of Malthusianism is ultimately not its postulates concerning the rate of population growth as such, but its presumption that the root of man's economic problems lies in his rate of demographic expansion rather than in his social and political institutions. It has been to defend their short-sighted desire to solve the food problem within the confines of the outmoded social-economic agricultural relationships which characterize most food-deficit countries, that the Bank, the United States State Department and UNCTAD have enlisted the service of Malthusian doctrine and modern agricultural technology. Their application of the latter to a small and isolated sector of the backward countries' agriculture has aggravated the rural exodus and its related social and economic dislocations. It now seems amply demonstrated that a growing mass of unproductive laborers cannot be supported by the labors of a shrinking number of enterprises in a capital-intensive agribusiness sector, so long as these urban laborers are unable to supply the skills needed for modern-day employment in conjunction with sophisticated industrial capital. International charity, even at the rate of 1% of the aid-lending bloc's GNP, appears unable to support a growing stock of human obsolescence or to buy off revolutionary aspirations with the palliative of "capital transfers" unaccompanied by definite steps to increase socially productive capabilities on the part of the mass of the backward countries' citizenry.

It is my personal opinion that if today's problem of international backwardness is to be resolved it will be because an automatic self-governing mechanism exists in economically healthy societies that inversely relates their rate of population growth to their income levels: the higher the income attained, the lower the rate of population increase. A precondition for attaining high wage levels, however, is a braodly based increase in educational attainments: labor seems to desire to increase its living standards and to strive for self-betterment rather than to reproduce its poverty. The moral check is much stronger than was imagined by Malthus once the laborer is given a reasonable chance for profitable investment in his or her own human capital. Over the long run, therefore, implementation of birth control will not come as an alternative to economic modernization but as its complement. The difference is not subtle: it is that between cause and effect.

In a similar fashion, international borrowing will have to evolve from a palliative to a complement of economic evolution in the backward countries for any meaningful advance in their status to occur. Whatever the failures of aid-lending in the past, they need not persist.

To acknowledge these basic principles is to assert that any failure of future aid-lending and the spread of birth control to bring about economic progress will be deliberate and wilful rather than accidental. The era of innocent aid-failure is now past: persistent failure must henceforth be debited against the account of the aid-lending bloc and the compliance of aid-borrowing governments. Given the political strains that such a failure would undobtedly entail, aid-lenders will have only themselves to blame if some final and irreconcilable protectionist break results. In this lies both the pessimism and optimism concerning future international aid.

## Notes to Hudson

[1]On this point the Peterson Report remarks that Eximbank operations "are designed to promote U.S. exports and only incidentally contribute to international development . . . " *(U.S. Foreign Assistance in the 1970's: A New Approach* [Washington, D.C.: March 4, 1970] , p. 16).

[2]For an elaboration of this strategy see Lincoln Bloomfield and Amelia C. Leiss, *Controlling Small Wars: A strategy for the 1970's* (New York: 1969).

[3]Four forward-defense nations received 70% of all U. S. military support assistance in 1968: Korea, Taiwan, Greece and Turkey. In view of the Greek colonels' treatment of their country's democracy, the official rationale underlying this military assistance appears somewhat tongue-in-cheek: "Each[of these four countries] is exposed to and threatened by the substantial military power of a nearby Communist neighbor whose belligerence may increase that threat with little or no warning, as has been the case with North Korea. The more than 1.8 million men in the armed forces of these four countries make a vital contribution to the military posture upon which U.S. forward strategy for free world defense in part depends" *(The Foreign Assistance Program: Annual Report to the Congress for Fiscal Year 1969,* p. 44, hereafter referred to as the AID annual report, 1969). Nor are South Korea under Park, or Taiwan under Chiang-Kai-shek models of modern democracy.

[4]Quoted in the *New York Times,* March 8, 1970. This report was written for the State Department by Edward M. Korry, ambassador to Chile and former ambassador to Ethiopia, in which position he made an influential (but never highly publicized) report to President Johnson on foreign aid policy in 1966. His 1970 report also seems to have been relegated to the closed file of history after an initial flurry following its release.

[5]A similar quid pro quo strategy had been discussed concerning a Russian loan, with the price being Soviet adherence to the kind of postwar world desired by the United States, but it was recognized virtually from the outset that the political terms laid down would have to be such that no agreement could be reached. For an excellent discussion of the political price exacted for the British loan see Gabriel Kolko, *The Politics of War: The World and United States Foreign Policy, 1943-45* (New York: 1968), Ch. 19, esp. pp. 488-95. For Kolko's discussion of U.S. food aid and the political-economic strategy underlying U.S. foreign assistance in the postwar years, see pp. 496-501.

[6]Detailed statistics covering the U.S. aid and mutual security programs during 1946-60 by area may be found in the U.S. Department of Commerce's *Balance of Payments: Statistical Supplement, Revised Edition (A Supplement to the Survey of Current Business)* (Washington, D.C.: 1963), pp. 150-71.

[7]The Export-Import Bank was incorporated in 1934 to provide financing for U.S. exports to countries that could not afford to purchase them on

commercial terms or qualify for private credit. Its operations have provided U.S. exporters with a substantial competitive advantage in the terms on which their goods are financed relative to those of other countries. Available data indicates that export credit, not relative prices, has been the major factor underlying U.S. commercial supremacy in many commodity lines, for price-differentials along cannot explain the evolution of U.S. exports over time. Thus England's Radcliffe Report noted the Eximbank's assertion that although its loans "usually are defined by the countries to which the financed exports go, the direct and immediate beneficiaries of these credits are United States labor and industry, . . . United States exports, not the Bank's dollars go overseas" (quoted in *The Report of the Committee on the Working of the Monetary System, Principal Memoranda of Evidence* [London: 1960], Vol. 2, p. 105).

[8]According to Section 2 of the act, "The Congress hereby declares it to be the policy of the United States to expand international trade; to develop and expand export markets for United States agricultural commodities; to use the abundant agricultural productivity of the United States to combat hunger and malnutrition and to encourage economic development in the developing countries, with particular emphasis on assistance to those countries that are determined to improve their own agricultural production; and to promote in other ways the foreign policy of the United States."

[9]About one half of the U.S. government's expenditures of these currencies is used directly by the Pentagon, the remainder by other government agencies and "Cooley loan" sales to U. S. businessmen. For a detailed analysis of P.L. 480 activities, see *Food for Peace: Annual Report on Public Law 480,* for the years 1965 through 1970.

[10]*Food for Peace: 1965 Annual Report* (Washington, D.C.: 1966), p. 18. Nor do P.L. 480 sales work indirectly to displace U.S. commercial farm exports or to increase the agricultural exports from the client countries, thanks to the special safeguards written into the act. "Public Law 480 requires that shipments of commodities made under its authority are not transhipped or diverted, that they are used within the recipient country, that normal U. S. commercial marketings and world patterns of trade are not upset, that suitable deposits of local currency are made to the credit of the United States when called for in the agreement, and that proceeds of the sale of food and fiber are applied as specified in the agreements" (*ibid.*, p.17).

[11]*The Annual Report on Activities carried out under Public Law 480, 83rd Congress, as Amended, during the Period January 1 through December 31, 1969* (Washington, D.C.: June 18, 1970, mimeo), p. 2.

[12]*Ibid.* p. 23, italics added (parentheses in original). As an example of such marketing efforts, the report (p. 16) cites the country's agreement with Iran to provide 18,000 metric tons of U.S. vegetable oils through P.L. 480, on the condition that Iran purchase 55,000 additional tons on world commercial markets. This helped to reverse the downtrend in U.S. vegetable oil exports to Iran (and hence displaced third-country suppliers and/or domestic Iranian producers).

Sometimes the commercial returns are less direct. For instance, "proceeds from the sale of Public Law 480 oils used to finance private sector agricultural and livestock development projects are expected to result in sales of other U.S. agricultural commodities such as feed grains and livestock breeding stock as well as supplies and equipment needed in constructing additional facilities for livestock and meat production, processing and distribution."

[13]"Usual marketing requirements," the report specifies (p. 20), "are generally incorporated in agreements, and are based on historical import levels. Commercial imports may be required from global (i.e. free world) sources, from the United States, or from a combination of both, and must be accomplished within the supply period of the agreement. Provisions are also included in agreements to prevent resale, diversion, or transhipment of Public Law 480 commodities."

[14]For a listing of the ten nominal categories of self-help, see *ibid.*, pp.53-54. Number 10 (the final) provision calls for "carrying out voluntary programs to control population," although how a "provision" could be "voluntary" is somewhat problematic. Not less than 5% of the sales proceeds are to be made available on request to the foreign country for family-planning programs (*ibid.*, p. 10). It is necessary to control population precisely because of the program's built-in requirements that population growth and widening markets necessarily entail a mounting food-deficit (through the "historical market-share" provision concerning purchases from the United States and its allies). Nor is domestic banking in these countries to be helped: P.L. 480-recipients must carry out all transactions through foreign branches of U.S. banks ( *ibid.*, pp. 24-25).

[15]Four countries accounted for 69% of P.L. 480 aid in 1969: India (29%), Indonesia (15%) and Korea (11%). Wheat made up 40% of the crop shipments (*ibid.*, p. 14).

[16] 1965 report, p. 17

[17]*Peterson Report,* p. 31.

[18]1970 report, p. 17.

[19]*Ibid.,* p. 1 (parentheses added).

[20]*Ibid.,* pp. 2-3.

[21]*Ibid.,* p. 85.

[22]Secretary of Agriculture Orville Freeman openly acknowledged the use of food trade and aid as a political lever in an important policy-setting article entitled "Malthus, Marx and the North American Breadbasket" (*Foreign Affairs,* Vol. 45 (July, 1967). "Our unmatched food-producing capability," he asserted (p. 584), "has strengthened our foreign policy immeasurably." Its first effect has been upon "the balance of power between East and West." North America has become a vital supplier of communist nations' food needs, with the result that their food deficits "are causing them to become politically and militarily vulnerable." The United States has supplanted

China as Japan's breadbasket, much as it has supplanted Russia and its Eastern European satellites as Western Europe's breadbasket. "Without our ability to generate huge farm exports, these strong economic ties could not have developed. In geographic terms Japan is off the coast of California. This is but one of the more dramatic illustrations of the value of a productive farm sector in supporting our foreign policy."

[23]On this and related points concerning the balance-of-payments impact of U.S. foreign aid, see my monograph on "A Financial Payments-Flow Analysis of U.S. International Transactions: 1960-68," New York University, Graduate School of Business Administration, *The Bulletin,* Nos. 61-63 (March, 1970), pp. 24-33. The Peterson Report estimates (p. 32) that U.S. aid costs its recipients about 15% more than going world prices. This high commodity cost and the extraordinarily high shipping costs involved has led some countries to withdraw from the U.S. aid program on the grounds that they simply cannot afford to purchase or submit to any more "aid."

[24]AID annual report, 1969, pp. 23-25. The report adds that "Difficulties arose because local businessmen--not host governments--do most of the importing of AID-financed commodities. These private importers act according to commercial motives. Their governments often had to use unpopular restrictive exchange, import, or credit arrangements to induce private importers to buy the less competitive U.S. products permissible for AID financing." The official AID estimate that this measure worked to benefit the U.S. balance of payments by only some $35 million per year seems somewhat low.

[25]This may somewhat understate the full contribution to the U.S. balance of payments. According to the AID annual report for 1969 (p. 23), "The AID program contributed a net surplus estimated at $242 million to the U.S. balance of payments in fiscal 1969. The 1968 surplus was $81 million." And according to the Eximbank's 1968 report (p. 6), "Repayments and interest on loans made by Eximbank and on export loans guaranteed or insured by it are estimated to have contributed over $1.7 billion to the United States balance of payments during the year." (See also pp. 11-13.) It seems probable that military aid added more funds, thus bringing the foreign-aid program's net contribution to the U.S. balance of payments to over $2 billion.

[26]The biennial aid-packages offered to Spain and Libya in exchange for air-base rights are cases in point. It was in recognition of this political service of aid that the Korry Report accused U.S. foreign aid of hilding too tightly to the position "that development assistance provided by the U.S. should secure political support for the U.S. on important current issues" *(New York Times,* March 8, 1970)

[27] *Hearings before the Committee on Foreign Affairs, House of Representatives* (88th Congress, 2nd session) on H.R. 10502 (Washington, D.C.: 1964), pp. 83-85. For an elaboration of this attitude see Mr. McNamara's Montreal address of 1967. Note too the Peterson Report's virtual rephrasing of Mr. McNamara's strategy (p. 7): "In the past, the line of demarcation between security and development interests was blurred. The United States faced a divided world, in which foreign assistance was justified in terms of

the conflict between East and West. Today all countries have a common interest in building and maintaining a global environment in which each can prosper."

[28]If Europe attempted to purchase American gold with its dollars, Mr. Peterson speculated, the gold-price of the dollar would be driven down in world currency markets and--so long as other countries continued to tie their currencies to gold (which would in any event have been unlikely)--U.S. commerce would gain a comparative price-advantage over foreign countries.

[29]*Peterson Report,* p. 22. "The principal advantages of multilateral financial institutions," observed Rep. Reuss of Wisconsin recently *(Congressional Record,* September 14, 1970, p. H8646), "are burden-sharing and economic expertise. Through these institutions other developed countries share with the United States the cost of providing development assistance, as other nations have grown in economic strength, our share of the financial cost has declined." Regarding the Asian Development Bank he adds that "while it is true that Japan plays a big role in the Asian Bank, that is good, not bad. I think it is fine that we are getting others to bear what should properly be their share of the burden, and if we can get the Japanese in Asia assuming a large scale development role, I think that is one of the more hopeful signs. . . .in terms of the Asian Bank, I submit that our diplomatists have done an excellent job in compelling (!) burden-sharing on the part of Japan." (*Ibid.,* p. H8649.)

[30]*Ibid.,* p. 34. This plea for administrative "efficiency" is the historical rationalization for centralizing authority and bypassing the democratic decision-making process.

[31]Willard L. Thorp, "Foreign Aid: A Report on the Reports," *Foreign Affairs,* 48 (April, 1970), 569-70. Merely to state, as does Mr. Thorp, that aid is seen by Congress to be "obsolete, outmoded and unrealistic, mindless a boondoggle, a giveaway by Uncle Santa Claus, and a bureaucratic maze beyond comprehension, consisting of waste, frauds, sham, friends lost, enemies made and hopes dashed," is to overlook congress's very real concern that what is happening is not mindless at all but a concerted attempt by the country's last three presidents to usurp congressional power concerning U.S. international diplomacy and strategy. In this struggle the Cambodian invasion was a great catalyst bringing the issue to a crisis. As an example of congressional dismay, Senator Williams of Delaware has argued that "First we sell arms to a country, then we send advisers to show them how to use the arms. Then we send troops to protect the advisers. And that's how America gets into wars these days" (June 12, 1970, during the debate on the Cooper-Church amendment to withdraw funds for use in Cambodia). Two weeks earlier Senator Mansfield had announced his intent to oppose all of Nixon's aid programs, on the ground that all such programs were potentially military in nature (*New York Times,* June 2, 1970).

[32]The Eximbank is already doing this on a substantial scale. In 1962 it "initiated the sale of guaranteed certificates of participation in pools of its loans . . . . The Bank has sold in all, some $3.5 billion of participation certificates with maturities varying from three to fifteen years," (1968

annual report, pp. 18-19). Participations in its export-financing are now also being sold to foreigners, thereby enlisting overseas funds for the promotion of U.S. exports.

[33]*Peterson Report. p. 14.*

[34]*Ibid.,* p. 6.

[35]*Ibid.,* p. 32

[36]*Ibid.,* p. 10 (italics added).

[37]*Ibid.,* p. 33.

[38]See *ibid.,* p. 19: "If the United States cannot reach agreement with other industrial countries on this nondiscriminatory approach [of extending temporary tariff preferences to all developing countries], it should unilaterally extend such tariff preferences to all developing countries except those that choose to remain in existing preferential trade arrangements with industrial countries." The report specifically recommends that quotas be dropped on sugar, textiles and meat—something highly unlikely in view of the present protectionist sentiment in Congress.

[39]*Ibid.,* p. 18.

[40]"Epitaph for Bretton Woods," *Journal of International Affairs,* Vol. 22, no. 2 (Fall, 1969).

[41]See the World Bank's Annual Report for 1969, esp. pp. 49-52, 72-79, detailed statistics on debt-servicing costs of the aid-borrowing countries.

[42]He is also the only World Bank president to be unaffiliated with the Chase Manhattan Bank. McCloy and Eugene Black (1949-62) both joined Chase's board of directors upon leaving the World Bank. Mr. Woods (1963-68) had served for some years as an officer of the first Boston Corporation, an investment banking house with particularly close ties to Chase.

[43]As shown in Table 3, World Bank lending operations (exclusive of special payments transfers from Europe to the United States via dollar bond issues) since 1960 have contributed about $250 million annually to the U.S. balance of payments on current account, mainly by way of Europe. Bank-financed goods purchased in the United States have accounted for some $150 million of this inflow. In addition, the buildup of World Bank holdings of cash, bank deposits, and financial obligations of the U.S. government and its agencies contribute a further estimated $100 million annually.

[44]For a bibliography of Catholic opposition see Eugene K. Culhane, "They'd Rather Decide for Themselves," *America,* 120 (May 24, 1969), 621-23. In *Communication Social* of November 1968, a monthly periodical published by the Latin American Bishops Conference, CELAM, is an

editorial rounding up world press reactions to Pope Paul's August 1968 encyclical *Human Life,* delivered just one month before Mr. McNamara's initial World Bank presidential speech. An illustration of the anti-Americanism already emerging prior to Mr. McNamara's speech is to be found in this periodical's editorial comment, "Where did the greatest opposition [to Pope Paul's encyclical] come from? From the rich; from powerful nations defending lucrative interests in underdeveloped countries." See also Abraham Guillen, "Malthusianism is not for Latin America," *Vispera* (Montevideo, Uruguay: March, 1969).

45"Review of *Partners in Development,*" SODEPAX (Committee on Society, Development and Peace), mimeographed (October 8, 1969), p. 11, parentheses in original.

46*Ibid.,* p. 7. Mr. Elliot makes the point that "Surprise has been expressed that the report does not challenge the whole concept of aid and does not point out that transfers of financial and real resources are not aid but simply redistribution in the way that a progressive taxation system is redistribution .... but at the same time, the report seems to take for granted that aid is largely designed to provide infrastructural investment as a precondition for private enterprise (refer page 16). This is, of course, the worst type of aid philosophy since it implies that the object of aid is to create lucrative production possibilities for foreign capital in the developing countries irrespective of the real needs and aspirations of those countries themselves."

46a *Congressional Record,* September 14, 1970, p. H8648, during the hearings on H.R. 18306. Loan terms generally seem to be hardening for United States subscriptions to international lending organizations. Thus Rep. Reuss observes that, "Looking at the Inter-American Development Bank in the early 1960's, the first years of the Bank, for every $1 of Latin American money the United States contributed $11 to the soft loan resources of the Bank. In 1964 the ration was $1 to $8, in 1965 $1 to $5, and in 1968 $1 to $3. Under the provisions of this bill, this ratio would be further reduced to $1 to $2."

47*Ibid.,* p. 5.

48K. B. Griffin and J.L. Enos, "Foreign Assistance: Objectives and Consequences," *Economic Development and Cultural Change,* 18 (April, 1970), 317-18. "If anything," the authors conclude (p. 326), "aid may have retarded development by leading to lower domestic savings, by distorting the composition of investment and thereby raising the capital-output ratio, by frustrating the emergency of an indigenous entrepreneurial class, and by inhibiting institutional reforms."

49*Ibid.,* p. 321.

50*Ibid.,* p. 325.

51"Nothing would be more menacing to world security," testified Secretary of the Treasury Henry Morganthau to the Senate in its 1945 hearings on the World Bank, "than to have the less developed countries, comprising more than half the population of the world, ranged in economic battle against the less populous but industrially more advanced nations of the west" (Senate Committee on Banking and Currency, *Hearings on H.R. 3314*, p. 11). Jose de Castro, a Brazilian sociologist, demographer and former president of FAO, published remarks in *CLASC*, the monthly organ of the Latin American Christian Workers Confederation, praising *Human Life* as the most progressive encyclical the church had yet published: "The United States imposes birth control, not to help the poor countries--no one believes any more in its 'disinterested' aid programs--but because that is its strategic defense policy. We must realize that the pill is North America's best guarantee of continuing a dominant minority .... If ever the Third World achieves normal development, Washington's 'Roman Empire' will disappear" (quoted in Culhane, *op. cit.*). This interpretation poses the irony that the more liberal attitudes generally espoused by citizens in the industrialized nations on the birth control issue have been mobilized to serve conservative ends in the backward countries, namely, as a necessary device to maintain a para-military status quo among nations, and to oppose social change abroad.

[52]On this point see for instance Joseph S. Davis, "The Specter of Dearth of Food: History's Answer to Sir William Crookes," in *Facts and Factors in Economic History: Articles by former Students of Edwin Francis Gay* (Cambridge, 1932).

[53]*Industrial and Commercial History of England* (London: 1909), p. 55. Mr. Rogers added that "Vice and misery, then, the preventive checks to the theory which Malthus announced, are not found to be preventive at all. Thieves are inconveniently prolific; so are the miserable .... And the curious thing about the whole business was this, that while Malthus with the best intentions was consoling the oppressors of the poor, with the assertion that the poor, though the sole workers of wealth, were the sole cause also of their own calamities, he did not take the smallest pains to investigate economical causes. But the fact is, that Malthus was a metaphysical economist, and the only prediction which you can make about the conclusions of a metaphysical economist, is that he is almost certain to be in the wrong." *(Ibid.,* pp. 60-61).

[54]Such a proposal is not new: as far back as 1961 a plan for an International Bank for Economic Acceleration of Backward Countries (then known as the "Forgash Plan") was submitted to NATO. This proposed bank was to be empowered to make loans in the domestic currency of the borrowing countries and to exert political pressure where necessary.

# WHAT IS idoc

IDOC stands for "International Documentation on the Contemporary Church." IDOC is a cooperative relying . . . on more than 300 specialists...on groups and centers in 32 countries . . . on members of key Christian churches and denominations . . . and on all who have taken religious and human renewal to heart and are part of a worldwide exchange of documentation, surveys and reports.

IDOC, originally established in 1962 to supply the Dutch bishops with background documentation for informed participation in the sessions of Vatican II, extended its services the following year to all bishops. In 1965 it was available to all interested in trends and movements within the Christian churches. IDOC has now evolved into what it is today — an independent, transconfessional and inter-disciplinary organization.

IDOC views the problems of religious human renewal as transconfessional and inter-denominational and *not* belonging to any one country. Thus IDOC is keenly aware that Christians of all churches and denominations, as well as people from different countries, need to know more about the common problems of the modern world — this "global village."

**IDOC International-North American Edition**
**432 Park Avenue South, New York, N.Y. 10016**